Sept. 22, 197

Happy Birthday, Tex.

With love,
Kathryn

Low Man
on a Gill-netter

Low Man on a Gill-netter

by J.P. Tracy

Illustrations by the author

ALASKA NORTHWEST PUBLISHING COMPANY
Anchorage, Alaska

Library of Congress Catalog Card Number: 74-81788
ISBN: 0-88240-035-5
Printed in the United States of America

Book Editor: Byron Fish
Layout and Design: Roz Pape
Alaska Northwest Publishing Co.

Cover: Painting of the *Dolores* by J.P. Tracy.

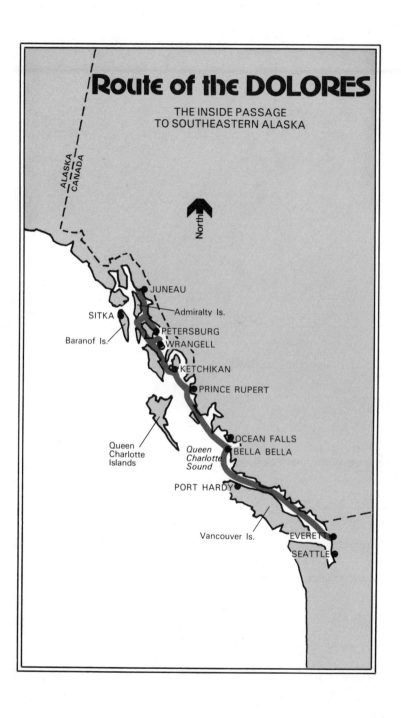

Route of the DOLORES

THE INSIDE PASSAGE TO SOUTHEASTERN ALASKA

ALASKA
CANADA

North

JUNEAU

Admiralty Is.

SITKA

PETERSBURG

Baranof Is.

WRANGELL

KETCHIKAN

PRINCE RUPERT

Queen
Charlotte
Islands

Queen
Charlotte
Sound

OCEAN FALLS

BELLA BELLA

PORT HARDY

Vancouver Is.

EVERETT

SEATTLE

Contents

Chart numbers referred to below are from
the *Marine Atlas,* Volumes 1 and 2,
by Frank Morris, W.R. Heath and Amos Burg.

Chapter One

HOW IT ALL BEGAN

Come in," bellowed Bert. He always bellows. After spending nearly 60 of his 72 years at sea, he habitually tries to outshout the wind and roaring waters even when in his landlocked mobile home, as he was now. "I'm already in," I said. "How you doing?" The old man looked up and grinned. "Ain't this a day for you? Never seen so much rain. Gettin' mildew on my feet, and that's no lie."

I nodded. "Warren was telling me that he's growing new webbing between his toes, and he's thankful. Said he suffered last summer when the stuff started to crack."

"Yeah," replied Bert. "He always has that trouble . . . well, most always. Year-before-last it rained all summer and he never had no trouble at all."

"I thought I'd talk about going north," I said. "If you're still interested. Seems like a good day to discuss it."

"Why sure. I'm planning on it. Toby is agreeable. We talked about it a couple times. He don't like the idea of losing his bunk, but that's just tough. You bet! We can have a real nice trip. Ever been to Juneau?"

"No," I said.

"Well, first off, we ain't going much farther north than we're going west. Wait a minute until I find a *Marine Atlas*...." He started to rummage through piles of papers and magazines.

"Guess I'd better dump a lot of this stuff. Here's an *Everett Herald* four years old. Must have saved it for some reason. Probably the weather forecast. Hey, here's the Atlas."

He thumbed through the book of dog-eared charts. "Here we are. Now see for yourself. And look at Nome, it's farther west than Honolulu.

"Of course Nome is colder," he mused. "But we ain't goin' there, we're goin' to Juneau. It ain't bad there, except in the winter. No, I think you'll really like takin' the trip with me and Toby."

So it came to pass that I went up the Inside Passage with Bert and Toby, aboard the *Dolores S.* An educational trip it turned out to be, if also scarey at times.

Having made my living as an aircraft pilot for some 40-odd years, I was in no danger of experiencing *mal de mer.* That turned out to be a blessing because the *Dolores* could, and did, rock and roll and pitch and buck—and she's considered one of the more stable vessels in the fleet of gill-netters that work Alaskan waters.

When I first met Toby and Bert, they were 84 and 72 years old, respectively. Being a feline, Toby's age was determined by multiplying man-years by seven, which made him 84. Both have one thing in common. They're really tough. The old cat is sort of nasty and Bert is just the opposite. Probably they get along together because opposites attract.

"Old Toby ever have any kittens?" I asked. "No," said Bert. "Of course not. He's no tabby. He's crabby. He's a fallow fellow who lives on crabs and oysters and salmon liver, and he doesn't like girl cats nor boy cats. As a matter of fact, he HATES CATS! That's why the people up in Alaska call him 'Terrible Tempered Toby from Taku.'"

In the military we learned that "rank has its privileges." Toby should be a rear admiral. He's a sea-going fractious feline who takes nothing from nobody. He rules the quarterdeck, the foredeck, the sternwell and the captain's cabin. While at sea he subsists quite grandly on succulent bits of calf liver, steak, crab, salmon and shrimp. He is a living example of the "RHIP" status previously mentioned, and he does not take his rank lightly.

A couple days after Bert's invitation, I drove to Mission Beach northwest of Everett, Washington, to look over the boat. It was mid-March and raining.

I found the *Dolores* and she looked a trifle tired. The rain and low clouds did little to enhance her outward appearance, and neither did the minus four-foot tide. She was sitting in some rather repulsive-looking mud. Rivulets of water drooled off the wheelhouse, and the remnants of a pair of gray long-johns flapped dejectedly from a rusty line. Her paint was scarred and flaking and the once-green reel displayed angular streaks of blackish goo.

My confidence was losing altitude at an alarming rate. The vessel reminded me of an airplane once owned by a friend back in the late 20's. He named his flying machine "Old Soggy" because it flew that way, when it *would* fly, which was seldom. So I looked at the boat and debated the wisdom, if any, of venturing north or west or any direction aboard such a splendid craft.

With a certain degree of trepidation, I crawled onto the aft deck, ducking under the dripping winter underwear. The house was locked and the windows were steamed to opaque nothingness. Consequently I abandoned further exploration for that day.

Somewhat later I asked Bert if he had radar on the boat.

"No way!" he said explosively. "I suppose them raiders is okay but I'm darned if I'll buy one, not at my age. Anyway, I use the depth indicator to double-check my position when I'm not quite certain of my location. Remember, as long as there's water enough under the boat, there ain't no reason to worry. Anyway, I don't go poking out into crud when I can't see. Some guys do. Sometimes they don't come back neither."

That sounded reasonable. I've had my share of problems with "them raiders" too—at 350 to 400 miles an hour instead of seven knots, which is the cruising speed of the *Dolores.*

"No," he continued, "I've worked over darn near every inch of water between here and Juneau and I've never been lost. I will admit that I've been misplaced a time or two. Guess that holds true for everybody that travels in cars or boats or maybe airplanes. I dunno."

"Yup. Even airplanes," I agreed.

"So, you don't have to worry none. Another thing, we won't be alone. A lot of us will be traveling together. We always do. And we can't all get mixed up at the same time.

"We'll go over to La Conner, Washington, first and join up with two or three others. We always figure that to be our jumping-off place. I like it better than fooling around with Deception Pass. Sometimes you have to wait for a slack tide out there. Can get pretty sticky if you don't time it right."

"How do you mean, sticky?" I asked.

"Well, if the tide is running hard and the wind isn't right, you can get into waves and whirlpools and overfalls that will turn you every way but loose. I don't mind telling you, I'd sure hate to have the engine conk out in that place. So we go by La Conner and sort of follow the ferry route through the San Juans. As far as I'm concerned, I wouldn't do it any other way."

That was how we settled our discussion on basic navigation. I figured the procedures must be okay. After all, the old man had been beating a path between Everett, Washington, and Juneau for years. True, every season presented new challenges, but he had been meeting those challenges for over half-a-century and was still around.

"When do we start?" I asked.

"About the middle of April," he replied. "Weather should be getting pretty good by then, although it might be a little cold and rainy."

Prior to departure, Bert spent nearly a month getting the *Dolores* ready. He had the engine starter and fuel pump overhauled in Seattle. He debated about tearing down the 12-year-old Perkins diesel and doing a ring job, but finally decided it wasn't necessary.

"Them English fellers build good engines," he confided. "You can have your gasoline rigs, they ain't for me. I don't think they're very safe. Every year a bunch blow up."

I presume that statement will be debated by many a skipper. Certainly the record speaks for itself. I know I'd rather chug along with a sturdy old diesel than some of the modern power plants that gulp gasoline and stink and leave me with the impression of sitting on a time bomb. Of course proper ventilation and bilge blower-outers and good care and maintenance all lead to boating safety, but like automobiles and airplanes, boats are not foolproof either.

Bert painted and varnished every bit of the boat above the waterline with loving care. He washed and scrubbed the interior and then painted that too. Finally he had the old girl hauled out and after checking the caulking, the propeller and the rudder system, he arranged to have her refinished from keel to waterline with red, anti-fouling paint.

"There," he said, "she's ready for another season. How about that, Toby?"

The cat nodded. He was ready too.

Chapter Two

EVERETT—LA CONNER

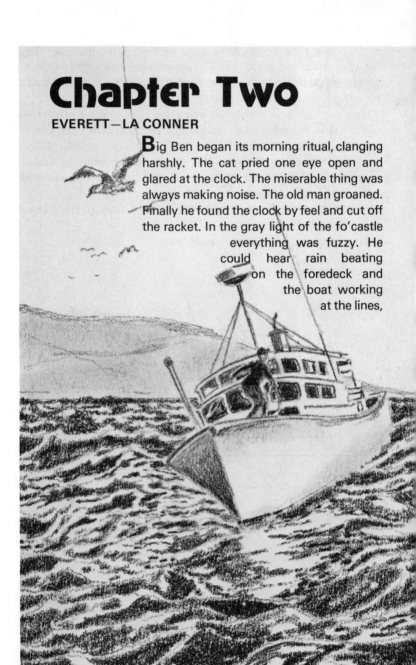

Big Ben began its morning ritual, clanging harshly. The cat pried one eye open and glared at the clock. The miserable thing was always making noise. The old man groaned. Finally he found the clock by feel and cut off the racket. In the gray light of the fo'castle everything was fuzzy. He could hear rain beating on the foredeck and the boat working at the lines,

We went back and got a line on the FLORENCE after the skipper called and reported his rudder had gone out.

complaining quietly. Slowly, almost painfully, he crawled from the warm sleeping bag and worked his way up to the little house. Still groggy with sleep he stared uncertainly into the new, gray day.

The cat sat up and spoke. They exchanged "good mornings" as they had for some 12 years. "Well, Toby," he said, "this is it. Another trip home for you. How about that?"

Some 1,000 miles to the northwest lay Juneau, a long and tedious journey. True, they would follow the Inside Passage but even so, there'd be hours of uncertainty. There always were. However, Juneau was home for the cat. His built-in homing instincts could have navigated the little boat all the way. He looked at the old man and grinned.

About nine o'clock the skipper of the *Florence* crossed the foredeck while Bert was cooking breakfast. He had to stumble around two boats to get to his own vessel. He didn't feel at all well.

"Hey," said Bert, poking his head out, "you sure look great. Run into another log last night?"

Art scowled. "No, I just had a dog bite me real bad, or maybe it was spoiled ice. I dunno . . ."

Bert laughed. "Speaking of dogs, that new electronic 'seeing-eye' of yours didn't help any. How come you hit that log?"

"Oh, nuts," said the younger man. "Probably you stirred up every deadhead in the bay, floundering in here after dark."

The old man smiled sweetly. "At least I didn't hit one. And you came in after me."

Art said something to himself and tottered onto the *Florence.* A small group of happy Indians greeted him joyously. Then he remembered that after mixing beer, wine and gin, he had invited them along for a ride to La Conner. He accepted a drink as graciously as possible and slowly collapsed in the fo'castle. The bunk should have been there, but it wasn't. Instead, he sat on a case of assorted bottles and cans. He looked heavenward. Receiving no guidance, he collapsed on the deck and swore silently. The guests applauded. Dimly he thought, "This is a grand way to start to Alaska."

The annual Alaskan pilgrimage follows a definite pattern. Two months before departure, owners and/or skippers begin thinking about house cleaning, engine overhaul, mending or stringing nets, painting and a multitude of such projects.

Two weeks before departure, owners and/or skippers actually start such projects.

Two days before departure, all hell breaks loose.

On departure day, half the jobs have not been completed, so the assortment of owners and/or skippers vow that they'll complete the work later . . . like next fall. They seem to manage it one way or another, because some 99.9 percent of the boats reappear each fall.

Our departure was from the Everett dock area and my long-suffering bride had driven me there, but it took some hunting to find the *Dolores.* From the parking area, all we could see were rows of masts. Boats of every size and color, scows, skiffs and yachts, packed in like sardines.

"There it is," said my wife, pointing. Women have an uncanny ability to find lost articles.

Loaded down with a king-size suitcase, a smaller case filled with tapes and film, and two cameras, just getting on board proved to be quite a challenge.

By ten o'clock on departure morning, Bert was getting itchy. It was time to start—past time as a matter of fact. "The sea-stores haven't arrived," he yelled. "Neither have Customs. They should have been here a long time ago."

The old man crossed over to the *Florence* and poked his head into the wheelhouse. "Hey," he said, "Hey Art, have you heard anything about our supplies?"

Art sat up. "No," he replied. "I'm going to call 'em right now."

"Okay, you do that. I just don't think we should have to wait all day. After all, we ordered the stuff two days ago. And now we've got the tide and we've got the weather. No point sitting here while those no-bets in Seattle mess around with our stores."

Art nodded. "I'll call 'em. I know the Customs people will be here if the sea-stores ever arrive." He got up and climbed onto the aft deck. Most of his passengers were sleeping quietly, smiling.

Shortly after one o'clock the truck arrived. Bert and Art and two of the Indians carried the supplies aboard. Five minutes later, Customs agents appeared. They checked the manifests and sealed the hatches. They were friendly souls who understood (somewhat) the problems of the commercial fishermen.

As an aside to the uninitiated, those who winter over in the Far North have a reasonably uncomplicated life. That is, life is reasonably uncomplicated if they have adequate shelter, a goodly supply of C_2H_5OH and a sufficient quantity of tobacco. Food, canned, frozen and/or dehydrated, also is considered somewhat essential.

For the winter-overers, the northbound fleet carries such necessities each spring. At Alaskan prices, one simply can't hack it unless he is living on and working for the local economy.

At 1:30 p.m. the *Florence* and the *Dolores* eased away from the dock, destination Juneau. Bert brought the throttle up to one-quarter and fell in behind. We cut south of the spoil area and then picked up a heading that would clear Hat Island.

The old man opened the windows. "Okay, Toby," he said, "go ahead and inspect the vessel, sir."

Toby responded with alacrity. He virtually flew through the nearest opening and scuttled around the little boat just short of Mach 1. There was so much to check, a fellow had to hurry.

We took one final look at the Everett waterfront. "Goodbye," said Bert soberly. "I hope I see you this fall." He turned and watched the *Florence,* then nudged up the power another 50 rpm. We passed the northwest tip of the island, the sun bouncing off the flat water. A few gulls coasted alongside, hoping for a handout.

By 3:30 we had passed Rocky Point on Camano Island and went bouncing into Skagit Bay. Whitecaps were forming as a westerly picked up rapidly, hitting 30 miles on the anemometer. Toby decided that he had experienced too much rock and roll. Without a word, he popped outside and beat a hasty retreat for the skiff. That was his personal haven when the going got rough.

For a while I thought I might join him. The rock and roll didn't bother me as much as trying to stay on my feet. "Hope it won't be like this all the way," I yelled.

Bert laughed. "No, I don't think we can be that lucky. Probably get rough when we cut across the Queen. But don't worry, you'll get your sea legs soon."

The old man looked around absently. "Funny," he said. "Art should be around here someplace."

"We passed him," I said. "You were back in the head. He must be behind us a little by now."

He stepped back and increased the volume on the "spook." The radio responded, hissing and gurgling. The old man looked aft. Way back, perhaps a mile, he saw a small white boat, rolling and drifting. "What the hell?" he muttered. Reaching for the microphone he called, "Hello *Florence* . . . *Dolores* here. Do you read?"

"You bet," boomed a voice. "I've been calling you. I can't steer this thing, Bert. My rudder is gone."

The old man peered back again. "Okay, Art. Stand by, I'm coming. Get a line ready." He came up and motioned me away from the wheel and brought the boat about. A number of loose articles went clattering to the deck as we pitched into the short-coupled waves. Rolling and grunting, we worked back toward the *Florence.*

"Do you ever call the Coast Guard if you break down?" I asked.

Bert spun the wheel three spokes and gunned up the engine slightly. "No," he said. "Like I told you before, we take care of ourselves. I don't mean I wouldn't call for help if I was alone. But we'll get a line on Art and tow him in. Don't need to go yelling for anybody else."

Bert circled the *Florence* carefully. He pulled ahead, then with power off, ran for the sternwell while the wind backed us down on the boat. He caught the line and took a quick turn to secure it. He opened the aft throttle enough to stand clear, with both boats wallowing in the swells.

"Okay," he yelled. "We'll go up to La Conner. Use your engine too!"

Art nodded. "Okay Bert, let's get the show on the road." He crawled back to the wheelhouse, hanging onto the handrail. Bert came forward and gunned the *Dolores,* watching the line tighten.

Once he went aft to check the line for security. After that we relaxed and let things bounce.

It was a slow drag. We rounded Strawberry Point at six o'clock then had a long wait until Goat Island was well to starboard. By the time we were ready to turn into Swinomish Channel, the westerly had abated considerably, but a new threat appeared in the form of menacing thunderheads.

"I sure don't like those things," observed Bert.

With the moderating sea, Toby jumped from his nest under the skiff and hopped into the house. He looked at us and scowled.

"Better slide the windows shut," said the old man. "I don't want that black rascal running all over La Conner after we tie up. And watch the door too. He'll try to make a run for it. There's a couple cats up here he wants to whip."

"I thought he wanted to go to Juneau," I commented.

"Oh, he does all right. It's just that he would like to leave his mark every place we stop and I don't want to spend half a night trying to find him. Ever try to find a black cat at night?"

There was a lot of lightning bouncing around in all quadrants by the time we eased into the channel, which isn't the sort of entrance one runs into at full bore. With the sky aflame, we poked along cautiously, hoping that a stray bolt wouldn't bounce our way.

We nearly had an accident just before docking, one of those unexpected situations that could have injured several people.

"Hey, look at that," bellowed the skipper. Eight young Indians, paddling a brightly decorated dugout, were bearing down on us at an alarming rate. For a moment a collision appeared inevitable, then laughing, they cut around us, intending to circle the *Dolores.*

Bert yanked the throttle back, fearing the youngsters would fail to see the tow line in the near-dark of early evening. We heard a yell as they veered off, narrowly missing the *Florence.* Up the channel they went, howling and laughing.

The old man brought up the power. "Boy, that was too close. You know, those kids didn't realize we had a tow. I dunno what they're doing out in thunderstorm weather anyway."

With running lights on, we made a wide, sweeping turn, bringing the *Florence* within a foot of the first available float. No question about it, it was a nice maneuver.

"There," said Bert. "I guess that will take care of Art for now."

We backed down and tied just behind him. Several people appeared out of the darkness, swarming onto both boats. I didn't realize it then, but they were skippers and wives and friends who would be joining us on the journey to Alaska. A few warning shouts prevented anyone from leaving the door open. Toby watched carefully, spring-loaded, but he didn't get a chance to abandon ship.

"Let's head for the restaurant," said Bert. "I don't know about you, but I'm hungry."

"Not going to cook on board?" I asked innocently.

He looked at me pityingly. "You'll get all of MY cooking you'll want, long before we get to Juneau."

Toby watched carefully, spring-loaded . . .

Chapter Three

LA CONNER — BUCCANEER BAY

Not even a ripple marred the early morning reflections in the Swinomish Channel. Bert sipped coffee, letting the boat loaf along at half-speed. Toby munched a few select pieces of liver and I shot a couple of pictures.

"Enjoy it while you can," said the old man. "We'll be bouncing soon enough."

We came up on the drawbridge that spans Highway 536. Cars were still crossing, their headlights cutting through thin ground fog. The *Patsy* was just ahead, waiting patiently.

At Trincomali Channel near Parker Island. The PATSY was running close in. "When I see such beauty and tranquillity, I can't understand why people bunch up and live in communities . . ."

Bert blasted the horn, "Come on, wake up," he growled. He chopped the power and we coasted down slowly. Finally traffic stopped as the center span commenced to lift, the control house riding high above the basic structure. This pleased me considerably. For the first time in some 10 years, I was on the traffic-stopping side instead of waiting for a cotton-pickin' boat. I could count on having to stop for boats if my schedule was off slightly when I had to drive to catch a morning ferry out of Anacortes.

While we waited for sufficient overhead clearance, Bert turned on the spook and called, "Hey, Captain Carl, you there?"

"Yeah, you bet," bellowed a voice. Most fishermen bellow — not that it helps signal transmission, it's a habit from long years at sea, before radio.

"Did you get a forecast?" asked Bert.

"No, I'll get the seven o'clock news if I can. I'll let you know."

"Okay. Looks good from here. Might get a few showers out in the Strait but I think it's going to be a nice day."

"Yeah. Well, I'll keep you posted. How's Toby doing? Ready for some crab, I betcha."

Bert laughed, "He had liver this morning and I've got some canned shrimp, so I guess he'll last another day or two."

"What happened to Art yesterday? Somebody said you towed him in."

"That's right. He hit a log or a deadhead going into Everett Monday night. Must have loused up his rudder. I dunno. Anyway, it come unglued out in Skagit Bay, so I dragged him into La Conner. Guess they'll hoist him out this morning."

"That's too bad. Hope it doesn't hang him up too long."

"Yeah," said Bert. "Okay, I'm out." He hung up the microphone as the *Patsy* moved out. Then he gunned the *Dolores* under the bridge. To the west we could see a Liberian tanker, high in the water. "Must have unloaded already," said the old man.

"Here," he called. "You steer this thing for a while. I'm going to cook some breakfast."

Obligingly I assumed command of all 37 feet of throbbing vessel. At each turn of the helm she responded by going in a completely different direction. I mumbled and grumbled until Bert stepped beside me and took the wheel.

"Lesson one," he said. "This is a gill-netter. The propeller and rudder are a lot farther forward than most boats. It's built that way on purpose. The whole idea is to allow room for drifting down on the net and not getting it fouled. So you have to lead the old girl. It doesn't answer to rudder deflection like the airplanes you're used to. You've got to plan 'way ahead. Lay in enough rudder to alter your heading and then wait. It takes time . . . see?"

"Okay," I said, "I'll lead it. Had a flying machine like that years ago. If you wanted to turn, you'd kick hard on the rudder bar and crank in full aileron to bank her. Then when she started to respond, you'd use full opposite control so she wouldn't roll clear over. Sort of a tight-rope operation."

Bert thought that one over for a while. Finally he said, "Well, the bacon is burning."

I wasn't too sure he got my message. Anyway, I started to out-guess the *Dolores* and pretty soon I was able to hold a course that didn't resemble a pretzel. It was more like a snake's track. But, I was learning.

We rounded March Point, cut across toward Guemes Island, then swung into the center of the channel. Ship Harbor showed up a few minutes later and I could see the *Klickitat* sending up a plume of blue smoke, getting ready for another day. There were several rows of cars, waiting to board the old ferry.

Bert refilled his cup and engaged the auto-pilot. "Might as well loaf while we can," he said. "Why don't you cook your breakfast now?"

Toby climbed up beside him and studied the water, which looked a little lumpy out in the Strait.

The spook grumbled, "Hey *Dolores S,* this is the *Tami.* Do you read?"

Bert answered the call. "Sure do, Gil, where are you?"

"Right behind you," was the reply. "Is that Carl up ahead?"

"Yeah," said Bert. "How's everything with you?"

"Everything's great. Looks like we'll break out of this overcast by the time we get to Thatcher Pass."

"Right," replied the old man. "I can see a lot of sun on Blakely Island. Should be a fine day."

So having settled such important matters, we went wallowing across Rosario Strait, everyone busy with his own thoughts, and I

Dodd Narrows. This should be hit at a slack tide if possible. The chart warns: "Flood, 9-knot speed. Ebb, 8-knot speed." From experience I've found that the chart is correct, and with a 7-knot boat, one has to play it quite cozy.

struggled with several pieces of bacon. "Should have cooked this mess before we got out here," I said to Toby, but he ignored me.

The *Evergreen State* was just backing out as we passed Upright Head. Then, after going by Orcas, we angled across to Pole Pass. A couple of youngsters ran down to the shoreline as the boats threaded through the narrow slot. Bert waved. The kids returned the wave and hollered something. The old man couldn't hear them above the growl of the diesel, but he smiled anyway.

The *Patsy* called. "Hey, Bert, let's hold up. Gil has some kind of trouble. I can't read him very well, so let's stop, okay?"

"Yeah," bellowed the old man. "What's his trouble?"

"I dunno. I think he said something about a water pump, but I'm not sure."

"All right. Let's lay off Deer Harbor for a spell. Maybe I can raise him. Will try anyway."

We coasted down and stopped again. It was peaceful in the little harbor. A few seagulls drifted over to inspect the new arrivals and an occasional splash marked the presence of small fish.

Bert got out a battered magazine and settled back. "Might as well improve my mind," he told the cat. Toby looked at the cover. Yes, the boss was reading *Playboy* again. The black cat went aft to the hatch cover and stretched out in the sun.

It took nearly an hour for the *Tami* to catch up. Gil reported that he'd connected a jury-rig pump and it was working. "Let's press on," he said.

The three of us eased out of Deer Harbor, cut between Steep Point and Jones Island and went bouncing out into Spring Passage. Then we picked up a heading of about 300 degrees and skirted the north side of Flattop Island. The tide was running fast, causing whirlpools and some rather substantial waves.

It took nearly an hour to get into the lee of South Pender. Toby grumbled all the way but he must have been getting his sea legs. He didn't run for the skiff.

We went booming up Plumper Sound and into Navy Channel. From there on things smoothed out a lot—until we got just opposite Active Pass. Then a British Columbia ferry crossed ahead. Between the tide running and the wake from the ferry, Bert had all he could do to keep the *Dolores* from jumping clear out of the water.

Toby jumped for the starboard window. He scooted aft and made a flying leap for the skiff. Sea legs are fine but this was ridiculous. He dug in his claws, cursing loudly. Fortunately he used cat language so we need not report his comments.

Coasting along up Trincomali Channel, we passed close to Parker Island. The sea was almost flat and only a few cirrus clouds marred the blue sky above. The *Patsy* was running close in while the skipper's wife shot some pictures, and I couldn't resist the challenge either.

"You don't get days like this very often," said Bert.

I nodded. "When I see such beauty and tranquillity, I can't understand why people bunch up and live in cities. Look at the *Patsy* over there. Anyone who could say that isn't a thing of charm should be keelhauled."

"You've got a point there. I think the good Lord was smiling when he fashioned the Northwest, especially the Islands. And He was very considerate in allowing a few people to see His handiwork."

The entrance to Northumberland Channel is guarded by a narrow pass between Joan Point and Mudge Island. The chart warns: "Flood, 9-knot speed. Ebb, 8-knot speed."

Bert consulted his handy-dandy tide table. "Let's see," he said. "That's Dodd Narrows and we're close enough to use the Nanaimo tides. According to this schedule, we should hit it right at a good slack. How about that?"

Toby had just come in from the skiff. He didn't know our position, but in keeping with standard feline operating procedures, he nodded sagely. After all, a cat is expected to look alert and wise and disdainful, so he did all three simultaneously. Bert appeared pleased. He likes to consult with Toby. Gives him a touch of confidence when the cat nods approval.

Pretty soon he called the cat again. Toby hopped up and pretended to listen carefully. "Up ahead," said Bert, "is the Harmac pulp mill. Now I want you to pay attention because you're always complaining about the mills back home. I guess the ecology folks haven't seen this one in operation."

Just then Carl, who was about a quarter of a mile ahead, asked "Hey, Bert, how's that for pollution?"

The old man picked up the mike. "Yeah, just great. I guess the Canadians aren't very excited about such things yet. And how about that monster at Powell River? That's even worse."

"Right," replied Carl. "Maybe there aren't enough people up here to cause any worry."

Gil called up from the *Tami*. "Hey, while you're all bulling, how about crossing the Strait this evening? Looks to me like we've got the weather for it."

They kicked the idea around for a while. It was about a three-hour run from Nanaimo to Buccaneer Bay, their favorite anchorage. "We can get there by 8:30 tonight," said Bert. "I'm all for it. Toby says he's willing."

"That settles it," called Carl. "If Toby says go, we'll go."

We bunched up and picked our way through Horswell Channel and after passing Lagoon Head, really poured it on. There were long swells in the Strait of Georgia, but few waves, which was a blessing. About eight o'clock a few stars appeared. The wind remained calm and the outside temperature started down, but not uncomfortably so.

"This is what I call a first-class crossing," said Bert.

Toby looked smug. After all, he had given the go-ahead for this leg and of course the crossing was first-class. What did these guys expect?

"You know," said Bert, winking, "there's a couple real fine tenderloin steaks in the box. How does that strike you, hey, Toby?"

I'm not certain, but I think the cat said, "I'd just as leave have some shrimp, but I suppose tenderloin will have to do."

Bert nodded. "By george, that's just what we will have and some spuds and canned peas and maybe a couple drinks. Sound good?"

Our three boats clustered into the little bay. With a clatter, we dropped the hooks and shut down the engines. Low wooded hills protected the anchorage. Above, the stars sparkled and danced in the crisp night air. A piece of the moon was showing, climbing over a row of snow-capped mountains to the east.

Bert mixed the drinks while the steaks sizzled quietly. "Well, Toby," he said, "15 and one-half hours today. Not bad, eh?"

The cat yawned.

"You know, it's funny," observed Bert, "but I'm convinced that cat really talks sometimes."

"I wouldn't go so far as to say I don't believe it," I remarked cautiously, "however, all he's done so far in communicating with me is to either scratch or bite me."

Bert turned the steaks and mixed two more drinks.

"Yes, sir," he continued, "two or three times he's waked me up and warned me of things . . . you know, like drifting onto rocks."

"Well, how come he didn't warn you the night you went ashore near Juneau?" I parried.

"Oh, I think that was my own fault," replied Bert. "I'd forgotten to change his litter box and I think he let us go aground on purpose. One thing for sure, he was off the boat and scratching a hole in the ground before I even realized we were in trouble. No, sir, that was my own fault. Never forgot to change the box after that, you can bet!"

Chapter Four

BUCCANEER BAY—SHOAL BAY

*"Hey, Thulin Passage is up ahead.
Maybe we can find a stray oyster."*

I 've been looking at the tide table," said Bert. "Think we're going to lose some time at Stuart Landing."

"How come?" I asked.

"Well, we should get there about three or three-thirty and we won't have any slack water until six o'clock. Probably just as well. We can get fuel and ice anyway."

Carl cut in, "I don't figure any further than Shoal Bay. How about you guys?"

Bert agreed. Gil sounded a little uncertain. "Nuts! Shoal is good enough for me," interjected Carl.

"We can make Cascade easy the next day and I'll tell you now, I'm not going across the Queen at night. Like no way. So let's play it smart, okay?"

We all agreed.

Bert was letting the old Perkins warm slowly. Certainly the engine deserved some consideration. It had averaged about 1,000 hours a year for 12 years, without maintenance except for two valve grinds. It rumbled evenly. He gloried in the sound and why not? It had never let him down.

He knew that one simple touch of the starter button meant the engine would run. No grunt, no grind, no groan, just an immediate rumble of power. They don't build engines like that any more.

"You can have your damn gasoline engines," muttered Bert. "I'll take this old honey." He checked the pressure and the ammeter. Water temperature had moved up comfortably. "Okay, I'm ready," he said to his faithful crew.

A thin overcast and calm water promised smooth going as the three boats poked out into Malaspina Strait. We picked up a heading of 285 degrees after clearing the shoals that surround Buccaneer Bay.

My drinking friends may be interested to know that some 15 minutes later we passed McNaughton Point without stopping.

When about an hour out, three gill-netters appeared to starboard. Bert studied the boats with the glass. He thought he recognized them but they stood off quite a distance so he wasn't certain of their identity. Also, he was unable to raise them on the radio. "Probably working different frequencies," he told me. "Well, we'll know who they are after a while."

Suddenly he felt jabbing pains in his left leg. With a curse, he slapped at the cat, who was sharpening his claws on the handiest thing available. The fact that it happened to be a human leg bothered Toby not at all. A good cuff in the face did bother him though, so he pulled in his claws and glared at the old man.

"You," said Bert softly, "are a grade-A, pure-blooded s------itch!" The cat nodded, ears back and tail twitching.

Bert cut in the auto-pilot and went back to the ice chest. He got out the last of the liver. "I should let the black son-of-a-gun starve," he grumbled. He cut the meat into bite-size pieces and gave it to his faithful traveling companion. He poured another cup of coffee while I fiddled with the little solid-state radio. After a while I managed to catch the seven o'clock news. A friendly voice identified the station as Nanaimo.

Canadian stations have broadcast policies that differ little from those down state-side. It must be admitted however, that announcers are permitted a certain latitude in their personal interpretation of the news. Sometimes one senses a bit of bias, but perhaps that is what makes newscasts more palatable. In any event, we listened and chuckled, and Bert tried to explain a few remarks to Toby.

There was a lot of snow on the hills along Texada Island. "Glad I'm not up there," said the old man. He doesn't care for snow, except when seen from a discreet distance. "Looks colder than a mother-in-law's heart."

The armada reached Northeast Point at 7:45. Bert checked our speed. "Not too bad. About seven knots. Guess this tide is running a little harder than I thought."

We swung to starboard a few degrees and angled toward Grief Point. The sea was beginning to make up into long swells, rolling through Algerine Passage from the Strait of Georgia.

Near Powell River, the other boats began to close in. They finally established radio contact and mutually agreed on one frequency. It was sort of old-home-week. The *Janeth,* the *Mabel* and the *Ginny Sue* all were rigged for gill-netting. The skippers carried on long conversations, quite unintelligible to anyone except those in the business. In general they discussed the previous winter, prices for fish, prospects for the current season and the status of each family. Additionally, they touched on new babies, old dogs, recent divorces, who was keeping company with whom, and a great deal of tremendously interesting trivia so dear to the hearts of friends long separated.

We hung to mid-channel while passing Savary Island. Some three miles of reef east of the island promised immediate destruction, even for small boats. It was just not a good place to go wandering. The sea had flattened completely and the sun was burning through the overcast. Bert tapped the barometer. It nudged up to 30.12. "Good," he said.

After a while he called, "Hey, Thulin Passage is up ahead. Maybe we can find a stray oyster. How about that?" Obviously the cat heard him because Toby hopped up behind the wheel and stared thoughtfully.

It was necessary to use a modicum of caution while threading through the passage. There's not a great deal of water at low tide and skippers must play it cool.

Bert pointed to starboard. "That's Lund. See, right here on the chart. It's a beautiful spot and believe me, it's really at the end of the road. From here on up the Malaspina Peninsula there ain't nothing but mountains."

It was all new to me, but Toby nodded. He probably remembered that somewhere along here there were some beautiful oysters. He stared speculatively to port. A few seagulls were hitching a free ride on a log. Bert looked at the birds and then at the cat. He didn't say anything, just grinned.

The *Tami* pulled ahead, cutting in near a large log raft. "Hey, Bert," called Gil. "Suppose there's any oysters around here?"

The old man picked up the mike. "Yeah," he said. "I'll bet there's a million—but we'd better not stop. I don't want any trouble with the law, do you?"

"No, sir," was the reply.

Whether anyone did stop is quite beside the point. The fact remains that all boats were accounted for long before we passed Kinghorn Island, and Toby sat at the wheel, frustrated. He glared up Desolation Sound, unimpressed with the breath-taking beauty. No oysters!

Bert took a pinch of snuff and shoved the cat aside. "If you can't steer, let me have it," he said.

Going up Lewis Channel the boats passed a settlement called Squirrel Cove. On Cortes Island, it sits squarely in the middle of nowhere. I counted 14 houses and one great big white church.

"I guess those Indians don't have much to do except keep in touch with the Great Spirit," I thought. Looking ahead we could see white water, boiling through the channel. It has some interesting whirlpools at times. Great hills rise almost perpendicularly on both sides, rushing upward 2,000 feet and at several points, Lewis Channel is less than a quarter of a mile wide.

For some reason, one may fully expect to meet a long tow at the narrowest point. Apparently this phenomenon is skillfully planned by persons unknown, but you may depend on it. We met a tow right on schedule.

"Well," said Bert, carefully dodging the aft end of some wildly swinging logs, "we'll be up to Yuculta Rapids pretty soon, so I'm going to put in at Stuart Landing, like we discussed this morning. We'll wait for a slack tide." Turning to the cat, he added, "Now, I want you to stay right on board, understand?"

Toby gazed at him much like a disgusted teen-ager asking, "Who, me? You know I wouldn't think of jumping ship."

Bert opened the window, spitting into the clear water. "Yes, you," he said, closing the glass. "And I don't want any nonsense."

At 3:20 the *Dolores* eased into the dock. The resort owner, Jack Howes, came bounding down the steep ramp and helped us tie up. The *Patsy* slid in beside, followed by the other four boats. "You gentlemen need fuel, water, food, ice or a drink?" asked Jack.

"Well, speaking for myself," said Bert, "I'll take 'em all in that order."

Carl said, "Seeing as how we've got to wait for that six o'clock tide, we might as well get everything done now."

We got our fuel and ice and other goodies and then climbed up to the Trophy Room. A few beers sounded quite reasonable at this point.

Toby managed to create a fuss just as we were starting to move out at 6 p.m. The tide was slack and there was real urgency in setting forth before it began to run again, but somehow the cat managed to slip out the door and leap for the dock just as Bert cast off the bowline. The deed was consummated in a millisecond, so fast that no one saw his dash for freedom. When

Toby and I munched a few oysters.
It certainly was a strange meal and we
tired of it quickly.

the old man looked around, there was the black rascal heading up the ramp.

Bert yelled and dropped the line. He took off on a dead run. When he hollered, the cat ducked instinctively, which was his undoing. Toby received a cuff so quickly and thoroughly, it knocked him right back on the float. He screamed and leaped for the *Dolores.*

Perhaps the whole affair would have ended right there had Captain Carl not been easing the *Patsy* out. Without hesitation, the cat hurled himself across some four feet of open water, landing on the aft deck, spitting and snarling.

Faye stuck her head out and laughed. "Looks like we've got a passenger."

Toby thought otherwise. To his horror, he realized that he was on the wrong boat and that his home was becoming progressively smaller. He let out a scream that startled several sleepy gulls and echoed up and down the hills.

In the meantime, Bert got the *Dolores* underway and came charging up, cussing a blue streak. "Jump, you black S.O.B.," he yelled. Toby did.

Carl called, "Hey, I was just going to collect his ticket!"

It's only 10 miles from Stuart Landing to Shoal Bay, but even at slack tide it can be a wild ride. We skirted Denham Islet and went slam-banging into the lower end of Cordero Channel.

"Stay north of Channe Island," called Carl. So we all did, and finally beat our way almost up to Godwin Point. Then a sweeping turn to port put us safely inside Shoal.

Bert got the hook out at eight o'clock. "Not too bad," he commented. "Ten miles in two hours."

Someone had put a pail of fresh oysters on board back at Stuart Landing. Bert wasn't sure who, but never look a gift-horse. . . As we went bounding around the channel, the old man popped a dozen in the oven. Nothing better than oven-roasted oysters. However, Bert forgot to turn up the stove. The result was an oven full of oysters that refused to pop open. Instead, they died a slow death and gradually charred. Somehow they had the consistency of salted rawhide and were nearly as tasty.

Bert pried several open, cursing himself, then mixed a drink and sipped it thoughtfully. Finally he said, "To hell with the whole nasty affair," and went to bed.

Toby and I munched a few oysters. It certainly was a strange meal and we tired of it quickly. The cat rolled up in an untidy ball while I opened a small can of beans.

Although we could never pin down the facts, it is known that somebody dragged anchor that night and went pounding out into the middle of Cordero Channel while sound asleep.

A Canadian trawler came around the bend and fortunately saw the drifting boat just in time. The skipper got his vessel into backup before he slammed into the aimlessly wandering stranger. His efforts to awaken the crew involved shining lights into the house and pounding on the side with a boat hook. Finally, as he was about to board her, the sleepy owner awoke. Naturally, nobody owned up to that snafu.

Chapter Five

SHOAL BAY—CASCADE HARBOUR

It was clear and cold at 4:30 in the morning. To the south-west, moonlight danced along the snow-capped hills and the little boats were heavy with frost. As the engines started exhaust plumes bunched up and hung in the still air like blue cotton balls, then the usual clanking of anchor chains announced a fresh start.

Apparently the burned oysters hadn't set too well. My stomach and lower plumbing had rumbled and grumbled all night, so when we arose my first move was to the head.

Bert quite thoughtfully had provided a circular opening at the bottom of the privacy door, to permit Toby to enter or leave at will. In back of the throne there was space enough for his litter box. A very nice arrangement, because thanks to modern technology, cat litter is clean and odorless (up to a point).

JOE TRACY

As I rushed into the little room, I did not turn on the light. The reason for staying in the dark is to keep one's night vision. This morning we would soon poke out into the dark channel with only bits of moonlight to aid in feeling our way.

In keeping with normal operating procedures, I sat down and immediately started the pump—then jumped a good two feet! Something shot between my legs, screaming and clawing, and nearly sent me through the plywood wall.

Bert yelled and yanked on the house light. Toby blinked and ducked back toward the toilet door. I started to laugh.

"Hell!" said Bert. "Now I can't see a thing outside. Guess I might as well feed the cat."

He opened a can of "Gourmet Delight" and smelled the contents. "Bet you it's just chicken guts," he said to Toby as the cat sniffed it. Bert poured a cup of coffee, snapped off the light and settled down behind the wheel, waiting for his eyes to adjust to the darkness again.

For a few minutes the radio channel was jammed with sort of a morning roll call. The cross fire ended as abruptly as it had begun but not before Bert told the tale of the toilet, much to the amusement of all.

We turned up Wellbore Channel at 6:30. At Carterer Point the hills squeeze the water like a Venturi, and wild whirlpools slam from shore to shore. Bert cursed quietly and fought the mad gyrations. At Althorp Point we picked up a heading of 238 degrees and went pounding into Sunderland Channel. This gave a clear shot at Johnstone Strait. The old man stayed in mid-channel, keeping Hardwicke Island to port.

"Looks like we'll be bucking a running tide," he said. "Here, you steer for a while. I'm getting tired."

As we turned into the Strait, waves began to break apart over the bow. Low scud was moving down across the hills and the water became a sulky gray. There was a lot of traffic. Near Sophia Islands we met an eastbound tug, dragging a barge piled high with logs.

"There goes a load to Powell River," said Bert. There's a big pulp mill there.

Another boat met us, furrowing out a mean wake. We bounced over a few and I tried to hold a course of 260 degrees as we passed the Blinkhorn marker. Bert peered ahead. "By golly, there's sunshine up there. How about that? Maybe we'll have some good weather at Alert Bay."

Passing Lewis Point at 12:30, Bert took over and nudged the *Dolores* to starboard a few points. Cormorant Island was clearly visible and he planned his course accordingly. Sunshine was bouncing off the hills and reflecting from the sparkling blue water as we docked.

Gil came walking back from the *Tami* while fuel was being pumped into the boats. He had a sack of smoked salmon and waved it. "Thought you might like a bit for dinner," he said. "Did you get the weather forecast? The guessers say we're going to have gale winds tonight. I don't believe it though."

Bert shrugged. "Me neither. The glass is steady and this north breeze smells like the middle of a good high."

"That's the way I see it," said Gil.

Carl finished refueling. After kicking on the fresh-water hose, he came rolling down the float. He agreed with the two skippers. "I'm betting on south-easterly tomorrow, just as soon as this high pressure cell works over the mainland," he said. "I know there's got to be a low behind it. Anyway, unless the crystal-ballers can do better, I'll make book on an easy crossing in the morning."

Toby was more interested in the sack Gil had given Bert than he was in the weather.

Gil turned to me. "I hear you got all fouled up in a cat house this morning."

"Faye heard about it too," said Carl.

"There's nothing sacred, now that you guys have radio," I retorted.

"Did you see the totem poles when we were coming in?" asked Gil.

"Yeah," replied Bert. "Some day I'm going to walk down there and shoot some pictures."

"Better get some film," said Carl. Then turning to Gil: "He's been lugging that 1918 Kodak around since World War I. Never has used the thing."

Bert grinned. "Well, I took aim on one totem pole but it was almost as ugly as you. I wouldn't waste film on THAT!"

The marine service lad stepped out of the shack. "Ninety-three gallons, Bert," he called.

41

The old man said, "Hey, even if that's imperial gallons it ain't too bad is it? Guess the old girl is as easy on fuel as ever."

Gil laughed. "No wonder. I seen a jelly-fish passing you back near Lewis Point."

"Bullmanure," replied Bert. They parted, each heading for his own boat.

Easing past Haddington Reef at 2:30, Bert noted the barometer. It had worked up to 30.35. A thin overcast was forming and the surface wind had dropped to a northerly whisper. "Still think the forecasters are wrong," he said. "I sure ain't got any arthritic twinges."

The sea remained calm. At 5:30 we were abeam Hardy Bay. Bert told me to pick up a heading of 267 degrees as we slid past the Masterman Islands. It looked good. No wind, no tide. "Makes navigation downright gentlemanly," Bert commented.

An hour later we cut in between Balaklava Island and Nigei and threaded our way through Browning Passage. "You know," said the old man, "we passed Hurst Island back a little bit. There's a small harbor tucked away on the west side called God's Pocket. Used to have service there but the people moved away, or died, or something.

"I guess that was before your time," continued the old man, looking at Toby. "Nowadays we go up to Cascade. Of course there ain't any service there, but it's a good jumping-off spot for the Queen. You can really look out and decide if you want to try it or not."

Two boats forged ahead. They stood well off from Greeting Point and then away out from Cholberg Point and with good reason. Long swells, the ocean-going variety that start in Japan and roll all the way across the Pacific, were laying in from about 300 degrees. Toward shore they were being broken and shredded into white and green froth, exploding violently as they collided with an endless variety of black rocks and shoals. There were no gulls in evidence. Even birds avoid this torn area.

Bert had taken over. He watched carefully, waiting for just the right spot to turn in and dash for the anchorage.

"We'll have to get out Volume 2 of the *Marine Atlas* tomorrow," he said. "We've run out of charts."

We dropped the hook at 7:30. Running time, 14 hours and 30 minutes.

The old man put some hamburger and onions on to cook, opened a can of beans and stoked up to heat the oven for toast. "By damn," he said, "I think we'll have a drink. How about you?" He looked at us both.

As usual, the cat gazed at him unblinkingly. I said, "Go ahead, booze it up. You'll rot your liver out some day. Pour me one, too."

While the meat sizzled and slowly shrank to virtually nothing, Bert thumbed through the *Marine Atlas.* He sipped his drink and chuckled at the antique data provided for Cascade Harbour:

"Mr. E. Brown has house. Does some minor hull repair. Dock is deteriorated. Closest harbour for anchorage waiting for weather in crossing Queen Charlotte Sound. Good anchorage but, slight swell may work into Bay at times."

Bert put the beans on to heat. "Nothing like being current with information to mariners. I figure Mr. Brown must have deteriorated right along with his dock, at least 10 years ago."

Carl brought the *Patsy* alongside. "Hey," he called. "Is there anybody at home?"

"You bet," yelled Bert. He jumped outside and grabbed a line. "Come on aboard and have a drink."

Faye and Carl came into the house. "Smells good," she said. "What you cooking, buckshot?"

"No," said Bert. "That junk started out as ground beef. Then I poured off the fat. Then I poured off some more—and pretty soon I'm going to deep-six the whole damned mess."

She nodded. "I've noticed a lot of fat in ground meat lately."

"Just the opposite," said Carl. "I've noticed a little meat in a lot of ground fat."

"Well to hell with it," growled Bert. "Help yourself to a drink, I gotta stir the beans.

We chatted for a while. Toby got out and checked the *Patsy* carefully, but it was getting chilly and he was hungry.

"Let's try for a five o'clock departure," suggested Carl. "We can be across in four or four and one-half hours, and even if the weather makes up, we'll be inside of Calvert Island before it can amount to much."

Bert nodded. "I'll buy that. How about you Faye? Gonna get up at four o'clock and make breakfast?"

She looked at him and smiled. "Eat your damned cat food," she said sweetly.

Chapter Six

CASCADE HARBOUR—PORT BLACKNEY

If you look at a chart of the Pacific Ocean, you'll notice that there isn't anything but water between Vancouver Island and Tokyo. The big swells that form over by O'Shima moderate somewhat as they feel the effects of the North American Continental Shelf, but even so they're still big when they finally arrive. And, even if you follow the Inside Passage you must cross Queen Charlotte Sound, 31 miles of open sea. That is where small boats can run into big trouble. A 30-foot boat riding across 40-foot swells can have problems.

The swells run west to east. If weather conditions are such that surface winds go in the opposite direction, then waves form and gallop from east to west. Our little armada found itself trying to

Crossing Queen Charlotte Sound—31 miles of open sea.

maintain a heading that angled across both swells and waves at 320 degrees. The swells were rolling in at about 270 degrees and the wind was buffeting the sterns from 130 degrees. The wide stern of the *Dolores* presented a great deal of area for wind and wave to shove sideways. Every time we fell into a trough, it was merely an educated guess as to bow direction when we climbed out. So, to quote an old salty expression, the ride developed into quite a "bitch-kitty," an expression that had nothing to do with Toby.

We had departed the comfortable shelter of Cascade Harbour at five o'clock, the barometer pegged at 30.20, indicating steady weather. The wind was blustering from the southeast at about 20 knots. ·

"I really don't like it," Bert said. "We're going to get the wind quartering astern, and this old girl is going to try to weathercock all the way across."

The boats were strung out in trail formation. As we passed the lee of Hope Island, the swells started to slam hard. About halfway to Pine Island the wind really grabbed the boats. Having a wide butt, the *Dolores* took the brunt of the waves. We could see the *Patsy* up ahead, mincing along with hardly a quiver.

"By damn," said Bert, "I sure as hell wish this boat was a double-ender, once in a while—and this is one of those times." He spun the wheel, trying to outguess the next onslaught. Toby went back to his sandbox and regurgitated quietly.

As the cat came back into the house, Bert looked at him and frowned. "Here," he said to me, "hold her for a minute." He grabbed the cat and hustled him to the door. Toby got the word. He leaped for the skiff, and none too soon.

The old man tried to hold 320 degrees but it was becoming more difficult. As we bounced past Storm Islands, the rolling and pitching got worse. That didn't bother him particularly but the pain at the base of his neck was making him ill. Every trip promised more of this damnable agony, and every trip lived up to such promises.

"You stupid, stubborn old fool," he said to himself, "go ahead, show the kids you can take it. Show 'em the old pros are smarter and tougher. . . ." He trailed off, grumbling.

He sucked in his breath and grunted as the boat heeled to port, sliding into a green trough. The breath went out explosively when a secondary trough rolled it still further. He spun the wheel into the turn as a runaway wave slammed from stern to bow, high above the windows, then white-capped into frothy nothingness, leaving the *Dolores* hanging on foam.

Time after time a following sea would burst upon us with a frightening roar, flooding the well and crashing against the wheelhouse. The sturdy little boat, built of oak and yellow cedar, groaned with each onslaught but shook off the attacks and wallowed slowly forward.

Bert tried a little do-it-yourself psychology on me and (possibly) on himself. "Boy this is a little rugged today but nothing like a few years ago," he said.

"How's that?" I queried above the roaring.

"Had to wait three days," he yelled. "Never seen worse weather. Damn whitecaps had whitecaps on top of *them.* Even the big ships stood down. We thought we'd never get out of Cascade. Good thing we had plenty to eat and drink."

A particularly high swell pitched us up violently. As we crested, I could see straight down into a bottomless sea of black nothingness. Bert spun us to starboard and gunned the old Perkins wide open. For an instant we hesitated on the brink, then, like a slow-motion picture, solid water came under, grabbing the boat and pushing us upward and back into reality. The old man slacked off on the power. "Like I was saying, even the big ferries waited out that blow!"

I can't speak for Bert, but I was shaking a little. I hate to get backed into a corner where I'm helpless. It's not habit-forming.

Carl called, "Hey, Captain Bert, how are you doing?"

The old man made two grabs before he got hold of the mike. "Okay, okay," he yelled. "We'll make it all right. Have you picked up Egg Island light yet?"

"Had it a while ago. Damn rain shower ahead now. We're on course real good though. I was able to check it before the rain. How's old Toby doing?"

"Okay your message," bellowed Bert. "Toby is back in the skiff. He'll ride it out. Don't worry. How's Faye doing?"

"Well, she sure as hell ain't cooking breakfast! No, she's doing great, really. Sitting down there reading a book and flipping ashes all over the deck."

Someone cut in, "Too bad, Carl. You reformed smokers are worse than reformed drunks."

Carl ignored the interruption. He had been taking such ribbings for over a year.

We bounced by Egg Island at eight o'clock. Bert observed that we were making excellent time, up and down and sideways, but rather poorly forward.

Another hour passed. Once I offered to spell him but Bert shook his head. It wasn't stubborness, just plain common sense. He was the boat and the boat was him. Together they became a single entity during times of stress.

The old man kept his teeth clamped tightly. The pain between his shoulders had spread to his arms and down his back. "If that southeaster would just moderate!" he muttered, "maybe this bucket would quit fish-tailing all over the ocean." He picked up the microphone. "Hey Carl," he called. "There's Dugout Rocks to starboard. We should be in the lee of Clark Point at 9:30. Okay?"

"Yeah, Bert," was the instant reply. "We got it made this time. How are you doing?"

"Great. Pretty easy crossing, I guess, but I can see a lot of white water up the Sound."

Another chimed in, "Hey you guys, get a load of the *Jonny L* coming up on us now. He's got a VW bug on the aft deck."

We looked back. A stranger was coming up fast, taking a lot of water over the bow. Bert and I watched as it went booming by. We waved. The old man said, "I've seen a lot of campers with motorcycles strapped on, but this is the first time I've seen a bug on the end of a boat. Hope he's got the car windows closed."

At 9:30 our little armada passed Clark Point. Four and one-half hours to cross the Queen. Collectively, the skippers began to relax. It was nice to be in the lee of Calvert Island.

Gil called. "We'll make Port Blackney tonight." Then he added, "Don't forget sunrise services tomorrow."

Rain was beginning to bounce off the boats with a roar and low clouds hid the hills effectively. "I don't really like this," muttered Bert. "Here, you work for a while." He went back to retrieve Toby from his nest under the skiff. "Come on in," he said. "You look like you need heat and a bite to eat."

Toby agreed it was about time.

"Hold about 330 degrees," said the skipper, "and keep an eye on the *Patsy*. Carl knows where he's going."

I nodded. It was still rough but the swells were behind us. Bert puttered around making fresh coffee while Toby rolled up on the rug. A most domestic scene, I thought.

"I guess I could have given you the boat back there," said the old man. "Maybe I should have. Anyway, I don't want you to feel bad about my refusal."

"Not in the slightest," I said sincerely.

"Well, that's good. You were an aircraft commander for years . . . and you always flew the plane when things got touchy, didn't you?"

"I sure did. I understand, so don't apologize. It takes years to handle anything that requires both brains and feel. And it takes a lot of feel to make this boat behave—which is something I ain't got yet."

He nodded. "Just didn't want you to think I didn't trust you. Tell you something though—you already have a feel. I can sense it."

Near Addenbroke Island the weather cleared rapidly. One moment rain, then blue sky. The sea flattened to an oily calm. We all sighed and relaxed. I cut in the auto-pilot and stood up, stretching cramped muscles.

"We should be up to Kwakume Point before noon," Bert said.

I noticed a sea-going tug, the *North Arm Express,* overtaking us. A red barge piled high with Alaska-bound containers followed, wallowing sedately.

At 12:30 we passed Namu Harbor, well hidden behind tree-clad hills. It was here that the famous killer whale was captured and named for the little village. He was transported to Seattle in a floating pen, being forced to swim the entire distance. To me, that was merely another example of man's inhumanity to creatures that cannot fight back. Of course, there are different opinions about that.

Passing the mouth of Burke Channel, the sea made up in a hurry. It didn't last long, but the unexpected pitching scattered several loose articles around the cabin, including Toby. He squawked and yelled until Bert shoved him out the door. "Hit the skiff," he growled and the cat did.

Near Addenbroke Island the NORTH ARM
EXPRESS overtook us . . . towing a barge
piled high with Alaska-bound containers.

Passing Fog Rocks at 2 p.m., Bert checked our speed. "We're really making time now. According to my calculations, we're nipping along at 8.2 knots. Tide really must be shoving us."

At Kaiete Point we turned into Lama Pass. Here again, hills ran down to the water with reckless abandon. Snow-fed streams appeared every quarter of a mile or so, falling and singing, heading for the sea. Once a huge flock of gulls and terns intermixed, all bent on attacking a great school of herring. The water boiled as the little fish leaped for safety from pursuing cutthroats, only to be seized from above. "That's a rough life," observed Bert soberly.

We swung up Hunter Channel, paralleling Campbell Island. "We'll be going by Bella Bella pretty soon," said Bert. "The old Atlas says there were 58 householders in the district, but I guess they never heard of the pill." In passing, we counted some 250 houses.

Gil came charging up with the *Tami.* He called the others, "Soon as we swing into Seaforth, I'll take the lead if you want me to."

They all agreed. Gil could thread his way blindfolded in this area and such ability was respected. We swung inside of Ivory Island and then slid into the calm of Reid Channel. It looked like a sheet of glass, unmoving and friendly. However, Carne Rock lies hidden in mid-channel. Covered at high water, it has seized many a careless or unknowledgeable skipper, tearing hulls mercilessly. We were glad to follow the *Tami,* cutting corners or standing wide as Gil maneuvered us to safety in Port Blackney. The hooks splashed at 6:30. Running time 13 hours and 30 minutes. Mileage, 101.5. A good day indeed.

"I'll cook tonight, if you want me to," I said.

Bert nodded. "Okay, I sure wish you would. I'm tee-totally pooped. Tell you what, you cook and I'll mix us a drink. How's that sound?"

"Like a veritable winner."

After Bert and Toby were snoring, I sat down with just a dim light illuminating the cabin, and thought of what I had learned in less than a week. One thing for sure, these fishermen were a breed apart. Certainly, they would try every trick in the trade to beat out the other fellow when they were working, but let one guy get in trouble and they'd haul their nets and run to help—under any circumstances. If a boat needed a tow or fuel or water or food, then that is exactly what he got. No questions, no discussion of cost, no growling about time lost.

Earlier, Bert had told me about losing Toby one day. It seems that eight boats were beating their way toward home. "'Twas a rotten day," he said. "Wind and rain and the sea running in every direction. Well sir, I suddenly missed the cat. Couldn't find him any place. So I called and told 'em I was going back. Maybe I'd find Toby swimming around someplace.

"Now you can believe this, because it's true. I turned around and then looked . . . and well by damn, the other seven boats had turned around too.

"In about 10 minutes or so, I happened to lean out the starboard window and right there on the deck, snuggled up against the house, was the cat. He hadn't fallen overboard, he was just staying out of the wind. So I called the guys and told them, and we all turned around again. Nobody said anything except they were glad the old rascal was safe.

"So you see, we try to take care of ourselves . . . even special people like cats."

I felt myself getting sleepy, and remembered the old song, "Rocked in the Cradle of the Deep." I climbed down to my bunk and shoved the cat over. He growled, then hauled himself on top of my stomach as soon as I stretched out. "Good night," I said.

He didn't answer.

Chapter Seven

PORT BLACKNEY—LOWE INLET

The alarm shook us awake at 4:30 a.m. In the absolute morning stillness we could hear other bells ringing on the *Janeth* and the *Patsy*. Bert crawled out of the warm bunk, fumbling for his glasses. Toby yawned and stretched. I just killed time, waiting for my turn in the little room.

Slowly, the old man went up the ladder into the house. In the gray light he could make out the *Ginny Sue,* the *Mabel* and the *Tami*, tied together, riding quietly. Lights began to appear in each.

Bert shuffled outside, shivering in the chilly air. He called to the skipper who had stepped to the bow of the *Tami*. "You going to lead today, Gil?"

The man looked up and waved. "Sure, why not? I might as well try it for size. And, a Happy Easter to you, Bert."

"Same to you. Watch that tide. She'll be roaring out!"

The noise of anchor chains, the grunting of power winches and the growl of engines shattered the quiet. A group of sea birds, shocked into wakefulness, muttered between themselves. To the east, the first light of a false dawn spread across the snow-capped hills and a pair of hungry eagles launched into the cold air.

The *Tami's* exhaust built up to a muffled roar as the boat started to move. Bert nudged the old Perkins up to 1500 rpm and eased into trail formation. He could see the *Patsy* just astern, the others lost in the darkness. I nibbled on a cup of coffee and wondered what the day held in store for us. Toby strolled through his doorway to the head, where the litter box was getting progressively less absorbent and required careful digging.

Easter Sunday— . . . the boat rolled . . . sliding sideways down a long swell.

Ahead, the *Tami* pitched up and over a huge swell that was booming landward from Milbanke Sound, then disappeared in the following trough. Bert gunned the engine to 2,000 and braced himself. With a groan the *Dolores* slammed into the first wall of water. Toby shot out of the head and threw himself flat on the rug, digging in his claws frantically.

Bert snapped on the windshield wipers as a geyser of green water exploded over the bow. He could see the *Tami* heeling wildly, then go pitching upward again.

He remembered the admonition contained in the *Marine Atlas:* "On either course going north from Ivory Island, exercise caution in the area west of Lady Douglas Island as, on a strong ebb tide, there are tide rips and overfalls up to five feet in this rocky area. Can be uncomfortable."

"It sure as hell *can* be uncomfortable!" he muttered, fighting the wild thrashing of the little boat. He slammed in full throttle momentarily as the *Dolores* tried to swap ends. Toby looked up and growled, then closed his eyes as the boat rolled some 30 degrees to port, sliding sideways down a long swell.

Bert studied the narrow channel entrance. It lay about 500 feet to starboard. There was no choice now. We'd be forced to ride the rollers and hope our center of gravity was low enough to maintain some semblance of a vertical attitude.

He fudged a little, keeping the bow quartering into the swells and watching his drift. Twice he thought that the *Tami* had nearly rolled. His stomach cramped then relaxed as the boat reappeared.

The first rip tide hit us hard, running wildly through the narrow passage. Bert played the throttle and wheel with consummate skill, curbing the wild antics, gunning into whirlpools, then reducing power as opposite roils tried to twist our little vessel and slam it into froth-covered rocks. Clouds of white spray betrayed their location . . . great black lumps peering out of the water between each long roller.

Slowly we beat into the lee of Lady Douglas and finally slipped beside Lake Island. Immediately, a great calm spread across the troubled waters. Bert throttled back. He relaxed and tried to shake off the pain between his shoulder blades. Toby sheathed his claws and stood up, shaking and ill.

Bert looked down at the old cat and grinned. "Poor old Toby. Didn't like that ride, did he?"

Toby sat up and appeared to say, "You're going to pile up someday, sure as the devil!"

The boats coasted along for the next hour, moving northward up Mathieson Channel at about seven knots. Fleecy white clouds played tag across the hills, breaking apart and reforming around the higher summits. Occasionally, shafts of sunlight cut through, bouncing off the water, bringing deep clefts and rolling promontories into sharp focus. A few rain showers stopped to visit the little armada, then moved off quietly. It was a beautiful and peaceful Easter morning.

After a while, Toby hopped up beside the wheel and howled at Bert about breakfast. The old man looked embarrassed. "Gee," he said, "I'm sorry. I clean forgot about it. Guess I'd better have some, too."

He asked me to quit making notes and take over. He went out on the aft deck and rummaged in the ice locker to find the last container of liver. He cut the liver into small pieces, then sliced several strips of bacon. While it cooked, he fried our last four eggs and popped slices of bread into the little oven. His timing was good. Everything was done simultaneously. Of course the toast was sort of a walnut brown and just about as crunchy. The eggs could have been a bit more on the stale side—but not much.

When everything was ready, I kicked in the ancient auto-pilot and let it clank and wheeze while we had breakfast and watched the ever-changing scenery. The diesel, into its thirteenth year, chugged smoothly and drove the boat at a comfortable clip.

Coming up on Jackson Passage, Bert unshackled the pilot and settled down in his seat at the wheel. There is a tricky entrance that must be approached with caution, that he calls the "Hole-in-the-Wall." It is well named.

The friendly *Marine Atlas* states: "A narrow S-turn at east entrance makes it difficult for boats over 75 feet and six-foot draft at low tides, or when the current is running. Run the middle." The Atlas is correct. Even a 37-foot boat seemed to fill the hole pretty well.

Once well into the passage, the boats spread out loosely. Hardly a ripple disturbed the surface. Green hills tumbled recklessly, and ice-fed streams fell end-over-end, finally splashing into crystal-clear water. Looking over the side, Toby could see small

Hole-in-the-Wall. This is a sneaky one. The Marine Atlas notes that boats over 75 feet will have trouble maneuvering around the narrow S-turn at the east entrance. How true! Even a 37-footer seemed to fill the hole pretty well.

59

fish darting about, almost within reach. Little did he realize that the fish were at least 30 feet down in the unpolluted channel.

As the boats cruised into Finlayson Channel, Bert called Toby. "Look over there toward Cone Island. Isn't that beautiful?"

The cat looked and blinked. Somehow a shaft of sunlight had bounced through the clouds and broken into a billion droplets of translucent color. The rainbow bounced off the southern tip of the island, painting the trees red and gold and deep purple.

It was nearly nine o'clock before we rounded the point of Jane Island and cut by the southern tip of Sarah. The tide was running fast and lots of trash came bounding around the rocky end of the island, causing Bert to dodge logs and an assortment of seaweed, boxes and floating beer cans. "Just like California," he muttered.

Swinging into Tolmie Channel, he whacked Toby on the back. "Look up there," he said. A large sign by the lighthouse announced, "Boat Bluff." A rain shower was pelting the cluster of buildings when a side door flew open and a girl, dressed in blouse and blue jeans, ran out to wave. Bert returned her wave and smiled.

The spook came to life as someone commented about the girl at the light. Nothing really serious. Merely a male comment about a female out in the middle of nowhere.

Near Quarry Point, our boats met the *Wickersham.* She was coming down the channel full-bore, leaving a king-sized wake. Bert swore softly. He turned and looked back at the cat. "This will shake," he whispered mischievously.

The *Dolores* hit the first swell quartering and pitched up and over, rolling viciously. Toby let out a scream and jumped for the rug, an instinctive movement. He howled as the boat slammed into six or seven more and then steadied down. Bert nearly cried with laughter. "That makes up for biting me yesterday," he said between spasms of mirth. Toby glared.

Butedale is a beautifully sheltered harbor, at the southern end of Fraser Reach. Unless one knows that it is there, it is quite possible to cruise right on by, little realizing that such a snug moorage is less than a mile away. Fuel, water, groceries and a coin laundry are available for transients, and the service is excellent.

A lake, some 1,000 feet higher than the settlement, overflows down the hillside, sending a noisy, roaring cascade into the harbor. It is wild and almost unbelievable. Once, during an early thaw, it overflowed and totally wiped out a Canadian cannery. Buildings, boilers, buoys and bidarkas all disappeared into the deep, dark waters, never to be recovered.

As we pulled into Butedale, the old man reduced speed to a crawl and watched the mad rush of water pouring into the harbor. "Wish I had some film," he said. "Must be a million gallons an hour coming down that mountain." Then looking back at me, he yelled, "You getting all this?" I nodded, snapping furiously.

We eased into the dock carefully, the *Patsy* just behind. Captain Nelson yelled over, "If anybody on this cruise drinks water, this is sure the place to get it."

Bert said "Hope the fuel service is open on Easter."

It was open. Two kids came nipping down the iron ladder and had the *Dolores* secured in seconds. They were bundled against the cold, not too neatly perhaps, but most efficiently. Bert looked at them and grinned.

"What a league of nations," he said to me. "Canadian-Irish-Indian-French and probably a Portuguese herring dragger to boot." The kids laughed and went back to secure the *Patsy.*

Forty-five minutes later we eased out and picked up a heading to skirt Work Island. We hugged the western shore of Princess Royal, hoping for a view of wild, spectacularly beautiful "Bridal Veil Falls." Perhaps that's not the official name, but it is to the old man. "Sort of gets a guy close to God," he said quietly. "When you can't see the sky for waterfalls, then you realize what a microbe you really are."

We went up the reach to Kingcome Point, then swung west again into McKay Reach, aiming for Point Cumming where the water dumps into Grenville Channel.

"You know," said Bert, "this has been one fine Easter day. I think I'll make a stew for supper. How about that?"

He engaged the auto-pilot and went rummaging around in the ice chest. "Boy," he said, "these spare-ribs should be just the answer. This will be going first class."

Filling a big aluminum pot half-full of water, he dumped in the ribs and turned his attention to peeling potatoes and carrots. Three whole onions went in, then a generous handful of salt and some bay leaves.

"There," he said. "By the time we get to Lowe Inlet, we'll have a feast, eh Toby?"

Toby refrained from comment. He'd rather have shrimp. Bert took two fingers of snuff and kicked off the auto-pilot.

"Boy! This is really living."

At 8:30 p.m. the hook went out at Lowe Inlet. Bert backed the *Dolores* down a bit until it dug in, and then cut the power. The silence was almost deafening until Faye yelled across from the *Patsy,* "What's for dinner, Bert?"

"Hog's end and spuds! Wanna come aboard?"

"No way," was the reply. "Sleep good."

"Now that was a nasty thing to say," I observed.

"Don't let it bother you," he replied. "Faye and me has been throwing friendly barbs for years. Tell you something, though. She can cook better, laying flat on her back with galloping pneumonia, than I can standing on my two, big flat feet."

After leaving Butedale we passed "Bridal Veil Falls" on the western shore of Princess Royal. Wild, spectacularly beautiful, the falls dwarf a man to the infinitesimal creature he really is. "Sort of gets a guy close to God," said Bert.

Chapter Eight

LOWE INLET – MARY ISLAND

The hooks were up at four o'clock. It was clear and cold and very dark. Bert elected to lead. He used the floodlight looking for debris, until we rounded James Point. After that he could see fairly well. The boats swung out in trail, poking along W.N.W. through the Grenville Channel. We had to make Nabannah Bay before the tide turned, otherwise our speed would be reduced to less than three knots.

Bert sipped coffee and relaxed after the sun began to throw light into the channel. "I went up here one morning against the tide," he said. "Not this boat though. An earlier *Dolores*. Anyway, the tide got so wild I was actually backing down this ravine. Managed to get back into Lowe Inlet. I'd spent three hours without gaining a foot, so that's why I wanted to start early today.

"Then there was a time I seen a couple Indians working their way up stream, and you know what happened?"

"No," I said. "What happened?"

"Well sir, they hit this tide running out and the last I saw of 'em, they was paddling their canoe to beat hell and they went clean out of sight, backwards."

We crawled past the light and we could feel the *Dolores* picking up speed. "Funny thing about this place," said Bert. "We just went by the point where the tides meet. Now we'll be going northwest like a bat out of hell."

After a while the old man called. "Come on up here if you want to see something funny. Look ahead now. Seems like we're going uphill. Do you feel that way?"

"You're right," I said. "Must be some sort of optical illusion. Guess it's the hills running right down to the water and the light bouncing through the canyon."

Bert nodded and dug out his can of snuff. As we passed a tiny cove, he said, "Look." Several gulls were skimming the placid water only a foot or two off the surface. Their reflections made each bird appear to be flying in formation with another, inverted.

The *Tami* was close by. "Look at its reflection," Bert said. "Ain't that something?"

We cut by Gibson Island, keeping Kennedy to starboard. "This is Arthur Passage," said Bert. "We've got to be very careful until we get into Chatham Sound. There's a lot of rock-lined waves in this area."

Finally in the clear, we picked up a heading for Lucy Light. "Now we've got some water under us," said the skipper.

We lazed along for another two hours. Blue sky and a warm sun was a welcome change from the recent rains. Toby took full advantage of the situation and curled up on the aft deck. Bert looked back at him longingly several times. "Wish the old cat could steer this thing. I'd be out there instead of him."

"Want me to drive?" I asked.

"Why yes," he answered. "That would be right neighborly." So out he went to sit with Toby.

Near Lucy Island, the old man came back in and looked toward Prince Rupert. He was unable to see the city because Digby Island cut his view.

He shrugged. "It's just another mess of houses and industry and people. Guess I'm tired of civilization. Was just thinking, it's been seven days since I've seen any TV shows, and I don't miss 'em.

He looked to the east and Rupert. "Good by, sweet Prince," he yelled. "See you this fall."

I turned up the radio just in time to hear something about somebody dying, but couldn't read it clearly. I told Bert, "Just heard a guy is dying."

He jumped and grabbed the microphone. "Hey, the *Dolores* here," he bellowed. "Repeat your message."

A faint voice responded. "Hello, hello. I said I was dying for a smoke. Anybody got any cigarettes?"

Bert turned to me and said, "Nuts!" He didn't acknowledge the transmission.

"How come you didn't answer?" I asked.

He shrugged. "Not one of our boats. Anyway, I haven't any cigarettes to hand out. There's two cases in the hold, but they're for Emmett King. He's paid for them. Probably the wrong brand for the guy that's dying."

Green Island lighthouse appeared on the horizon. "Time for my annual visitors," Bert called. Sure enough, within a few minutes five porpoises zoomed by the *Dolores.* They dove and rolled and jumped around the bow. Bert waved and talked to them.

"Nice to see you fellows," he yelled. They rolled into tight formation, less than 20 feet ahead. The old man laughed. These friends had welcomed him every year, ever since he'd started fishing the northern waters.

At 2:30 we passed Green Island light. "I never did figure why this rock was called green. Maybe it's the kelp around the low-water mark," said Bert.

As we went by Holiday Island he called, "We've got just five miles more to get into U.S. waters again. See, right here on the chart."

About five o'clock we went by Tree Point and started up Revillagigedo Channel. Bert was getting sleepy and tired. "Tell

At 2:30 we passed Green Island light.
"I never did figure why this rock was called
green. Maybe it's the kelp around the
low-water mark."

you what," he said, "you sit here and steer while I walk around for a while." He stood up, trying to shake off his lethargy. He toyed with the idea of making a drink. "No," he said, "all that will do is make me sleepier."

At that moment, the *Dolores* pitched up sharply, nearly sending him to his knees. He grabbed for the table, fighting to regain his footing. "What the sweet hell," he bellowed. "Why didn't you sing out when we met that big one?"

Toby had deserted his post with the first bounce. He lay on the floor, claws in the rug and ears back, growling.

Bert watched the ferry, the *Taku*, sliding astern. "I didn't see her coming," he muttered.

At 10 minutes of seven we saw the Mary Island light. With a brassy sea and a no-wind condition, we were humming along beautifully. "We'll be at the anchorage in a few minutes," he told the cat. "Just relax and I'll open up some shrimp for you."

I looked up the description of our projected anchorage in the Atlas. "Mary Island. Bight on N end of island gives fair holding bottom. Good coming south under adverse conditions." That cryptic remark puzzled me a little and Bert wasn't too sure about the comment either.

"I dunno," he said. "I've anchored here for about 20 years, going *both* directions."

The little armada formed a tight group as the hooks went splashing. Bert looked at his watch. "Sixteen hours today," he said. "No wonder I'm tired. Now, you black rascal, you get your shrimp and I'm going to build us a big double, double drink. How about that?"

For once, we were all tied together and this led to some visiting, really the first since our departure. Being a sneaky type, I attempted to tape a few tall tales. It didn't work. Too many people and, as noted earlier, all fishermen yell. My little tape recorder couldn't distinguish one voice from another.

The happy hour didn't last long. Everyone was tired and half-irritable and a couple of drinks reacted quickly. For once, I was in the sack before Bert. As a matter of fact, I didn't even hear him come back aboard. And apparently Toby was tired also. He did not inspect each of the boats.

Chapter Nine

MARY ISLAND — KETCHIKAN — BUSHY ISLAND

A cold rain greeted the weary travelers as we got under way at five o'clock in the morning. Visibility was about three miles and a gray chop promised some uncomfortable hours ahead.

"You've got to change that cat litter," I growled. "The head is beginning to smell."

Bert laughed for a while, then said, "Okay, old buddy. I'll get some fresh litter in Ketchikan. There's plenty in the hold but it's all covered up with groceries. But I do agree, the head really stinks."

We pulled in for fuel and water, close to
the Coast Guard station.

73

Knowing the waters thoroughly, the old man cut between Hog Rocks and Walker Island. Certainly that wasn't the recommended route, but was a good time-saver for the professionals. The water was full of trash, and a swirling chop made it difficult to see. Twice, Bert nearly collided with free-floating logs. He called the other boats and warned them of the debris.

"This is your friendly tour guide," he said. "Watch out for this stuff. There's logs and deadheads all over the place." However, by the time we got to Bold Island the water was clean again and Ketchikan was only an hour ahead.

We cut north of Pennock Island, staying in mid-channel until nearly up to the city. An automobile went speeding along the shore drive. "That's the first moving vehicle we've seen in eight days," Bert commented. "See how quick you forget about such things."

Bert pulled in for fuel, close to the Coast Guard Station. "Now look," he said to Toby, "I don't want any of your smart tricks. You just stay put! You hear?"

Toby ignored him.

"Another thing," the old man continued, "I'm going up to Customs. You know damn well I have to clear with them. So while I'm gone I'm going to lock the cabin and I don't want any of your howling. Understand?"

The cat continued to ignore him. He knew that tone of voice.

We completed fueling, took on fresh water and buttoned up the boat. The rain had stopped but the dock area was slippery and treacherous. We had to watch our step carefully. The low tide meant a 22-foot climb to solid ground, and Bert and I were both puffing by the time we reached the top.

Walking uncertainly toward the post office, I felt as though the muddy street were swaying. Bert also stopped and waited for his ear canals to steady down. "No point in staggering this early in the day," he observed.

The Customs people were friendly enough. No, we didn't have any booze to declare. No, we had not purchased anything in Canada except fuel. Yes, we were both American citizens and yes, Bert had his ship's papers.

The agent fixed me with an official stare. "What is your destination?"

I replied somewhat giddily, "Well, if we don't sink or get lost, I sort of plan on Juneau—or I *think* we're going to Juneau."

He thought that one over carefully. Finally, "Juneau, huh? Are you a crew member?"

Bert interceded quickly. "Yeah, he's the cook."

"You sure you're not a fisherman?" the man asked suspiciously.

"No," I replied. "If I was, we'd be skunked already, what with my luck."

"Hmmm. I'll put you down as a cook. Are you sure you're an American citizen?"

"Reasonably sure," I said, handing him my military ID card.

He studied it for a while. "Air Force. I was in the Navy myself. Never did care for flying."

"That's a shame," I replied. "I'll bet the Air Force could have used you."

He stamped the papers and waved us away. Bert took his copies. "Never know when you'll need them," he confided. "The Fish and Game boys will be checking, you can bet, although why, I'm not sure. This stop with Customs takes care of official registry and entry."

"Gives the lads something to do," I said.

Staggering a trifle, we dropped in on the nearest oasis. "Funny thing," said Bert to the bartender. "Every time I get to Ketchikan, I get land-sickness. As soon as I get back to the boat, though, I'm all right. Never been sea-sick in my life."

The man nodded, placing a fresh beer (at 85 cents a glass) on the bar.

We went out onto the muddy street again and picked our way back to the *Dolores.* "Guess I'll go down to Paul Hansen's for some smoked black cod," Bert said.

We cast off and worked around past the Coast Guard cutter to tie up at the store. "Now," muttered the old man, "I've got to climb another damn ramp. Should have come in here at high tide."

"Hansen Company Supplies" always smells good. There are racks of foul-weather gear, T-shirts and pantyhose, all intermixed. Then there are shelves of canned goods and cold boxes full of meat, fish and vegetables. Bert bought a package of kitty-litter, some new orange gloves and a big slab of black cod. "We'll eat good tonight!" he told the clerk.

The young fellow nodded. "I guess you will. Personally I can't stand fish. My mother used to give me cod-liver oil. Now I wouldn't eat one of the slimy things for all the tea in Tibet."

"I never liked cod-liver oil neither," said Bert. He picked up a new tide table, courtesy of Mr. Hansen, and went back down the long ramp. Toby sniffed at the package of fish. No, that wasn't quite what he had in mind. "You're a spoiled brat," said Bert. "Spoiled rotten!"

After a while the *Patsy* came poking alongside. Carl yelled, "Ready to go?" Bert nodded. He already had both lines off, so he gunned us up a bit and slid in behind. He waved to Faye and held up the package of smoked cod. "Remember, you've got to cook it," he bellowed. She laughed.

We cut around the red channel marker and picked up a westerly heading. Bert pointed to the opposite shore where the new Ketchikan airport was being built. The contractor had literally whittled off a mountain, cutting it down to a firm, flat base. Millions of tons of gray-green rock, blasted and broken and pulverized into workable size, had been used for runways, taxi-ways, overruns and banks. "Damndest thing I've seen in years," he told me. "Sure will be one hell of a fine airdrome."

"Just off-hand, I'd say its on the wrong side of the channel," I commented.

"Right! But, they've got some smart cookies working on the problem. I understand they're going to build a tunnel across. How about that?"

Just then we both ducked instinctively. A Cessna bounced out of the water to starboard. For a second it looked as though the floats were coming right through the house.

"Look out, you fathead," Bert yelled. Then a Grumman Goose came booming in, clearing the *Dolores* by a good 10 feet. "You too!" he bellowed.

Carl called back. "Hey, this is sure big business. I don't think I'd want to live here. Too damn noisy."

"Yeah," replied Bert. "Just look on shore back there. Ain't room to tie up any place, with all them floatplanes. I'll be glad to get to Taku Harbor where things are quiet."

About noon we passed Guard Island and headed for Caamano Point. The other four boats strung out in back, chatting between themselves. "Think we're going to lose our traveling companions pretty soon," said Bert to Carl.

"Right," was the reply. "I guess they are planning to head up into the Wrangell area. I never did any good in those waters, but maybe I didn't know them very well."

"Me neither," answered Bert. "Anyway, I sure wouldn't trade our spot for theirs."

Passing Ship Island at 1:20, our two boats headed out across Clarence Strait, 27 miles of open water to Point Stanhope. Bert and Carl chatted briefly with the others, wishing them a good fishing season, and watched as the little boats disappeared into Ernest Sound.

The old man built a sandwich of deviled ham, peanut butter and dill pickles. He washed it down with milk. Then he hurriedly mixed two seltzer tablets with water. "That wasn't very good," he confided.

He called the cat and asked him to come and sit at the wheel. "Over there is Prince of Wales Island," he said, pointing vaguely to the southwest. "See, here it is on the chart. I sure wonder about some of the early explorers and settlers. Here's a good one, Nipple Butte. How about that? And three miles away is Barren Mountain. Boy, there must have been some crazy goings-on in them days."

The cat wasn't overly impressed. To make his point, he bit Bert and jumped for the deck.

"That makes up for stepping on his tail last night," I said.

By mid-afternoon we plowed past Ratz Harbor. There was a good tide shoving us along and the sea remained calm except for long swells.

"What time you estimating Bushy Island?" asked Carl on the spook.

Bert stirred himself. "Glad you called. I was damn near asleep. What was that you said?"

"What's your estimate for Bushy?"

"Gee, I dunno. Where are we?"

"I'm not sure," said Carl. "I've been sleeping and Faye has been steering. I think that's Stanhope about 10 points to starboard. If it ain't, we're lost."

Leaving Ketchikan we cut around the channel marker and picked up a westerly heading.

"Wait a minute," Bert replied. "I'll check with Toby." There was a brief pause, then, "Okay, we're on course. I'll gamble on three more hours. How does that sound?"

"Yeah, that's about right. Thank Toby for us, will you?"

We dozed and made small attempts to stay awake. Finally Bert let the auto-pilot steer while he concocted a pot of his famous coffee. Having the firmness of syrup, one cup quickly brought him back to reality.

Passing the light at Nesbitt Reef, Bert cut in sharply toward Shrubby Island, and hugged the shoreline. The sea had turned brassy under a broken cloud layer, and only slow swells disturbed the steady progress of the *Dolores.*

"I wouldn't crowd that too much," called Carl.

"No sweat," replied Bert, flipping on the depth indicator. Then to himself, "Whoops, I need more water than this!" He swung the boat hard to starboard and we went wallowing out into the channel.

We rounded the north tip of Bushy Island and coasted into the little harbor, where we tied together. We got the anchors into some good mud and relaxed. The time was 8:10 p.m. Another good day.

"Now for some black cod," said Bert. He yelled across, "You going to cook the fish, Faye?"

"No," she answered. "Captain Nelson just volunteered."

Within half an hour the cod was cooked. Bert said, "That's the most delicious fish in the world. Don't know how you do it."

"You ain't tasted it yet," Carl said, putting generous portions on each plate.

Faye observed, "Praise keeps the cook happy."

"Right," replied Carl. "Another thing, you should always delay a meal. Then everybody is so hungry, anything tastes good."

"Hey," yelled Bert. "I've got a bottle of wine here someplace." He rummaged around and finally came up with a square bottle.

"Look at that. Nineteen thirty-six! Boy, that was a good year."

"Yeah," said Carl. "That was the year of the big salmon run in Skagit Bay."

Chapter Ten

BUSHY ISLAND—PETERSBURG

The old man had to get up three times during the night. "Must have been that bottle of wine. Had the damn stuff since 1936. Should have been well aged by now."

Bert set the battered coffee can on the floor and slowly climbed back in his sleeping bag. Toby landed on top of him with a thump. "Get off, you black bum!" yelled Bert, shoving the cat onto the opposite bunk, where he promptly landed on me like a ton of scratching fur. Bert pulled the bag around his shoulders, muttering. "That cat is getting nuttier all the time." Up to then I had been sleeping peacefully, but the rude awakening ruined the rest of the night.

We were ready to start at five o'clock. Even in the anchorage, the sea was choppy and as sullen as the sky. A dropping barometer suggested a change for the worse.

"Don't look very good," said Carl.

Bert shrugged. "No, it ain't. One thing for sure, the way the weather is making up I certainly don't want to be caught in this pocket. I know several guys who tried to ride out a storm in here and got dragged clean ashore." He looked across Snow Passage. "I'm figuring on a rough ride but, let's get it over with. We'll be okay once we get into the narrows."

Faye came out of the warm wheelhouse. "Brrr," she said. "Let's go back south for another month or two." She ducked inside again.

While we were getting the anchors up and stowed, Toby considered visiting the *Patsy.* He hopped outside, took one deep breath and shot back into his own warm house.

For two hours we fought our way toward Point Alexander. It was a miserably uncomfortable ride. A northeast wind, kicking up some 30 knots, produced quartering swells that frightened the cat, battered the boats and made both skippers angry. After we passed the point at 7:15 a.m., the quartering swells pursued us for nearly a mile, riding right up the narrows, colliding violently with the wild tide and tearing the water into whirlpools and overfalls.

Finally, as the water calmed, Bert called: "How's Faye doing?"

"Great. No problem. She's just starting to make some fresh coffee. We spilled ours coming across. Want some?"

"We've got ours on too," said the old man. "I'm going to have the cook steer this bucket for a minute and see if I can get Toby out of the skiff."

He retrieved the cat then scooped up papers, charts, magazines and the clock from underfoot. "What a mess," he muttered. "Good thing we didn't roll any further. Would have spilled the spice shelf."

He told me to throttle back a little. Carl was threading the *Patsy* into a hairpin turn, passing Midway Rock, and the old man wanted a little more maneuvering room between the boats.

The cold rain continued, cutting visibility and hiding all but the nearest channel markers. "I do believe it's going to snow pretty soon," said Bert. "If it don't, it sure as hell will miss a good chance."

As we passed No Thorofare Point, Bert saw a boat coming up fast. "You'd better slow down," he said, and watched as the stranger closed in rapidly.

At Beecher Pass the channel widened a little, just enough for the *Melanie Ann* to power up and run by. She kicked up a substantial wake, tossing us around like chips. Toby jumped for the window. It was closed. He yelled and demanded to be let out.

"No way," laughed Bert. "That's just a wake. Now get down and stop your foolishness."

"That guy must be in a hurry," bellowed Carl.

"Or we're a little slow," Bert answered.

The tides met at Finger Point. "Hey, now we'll be going downhill," said Bert, taking over the wheel. Soon we could see the *Dolores* picking up speed but the narrow channel kept us changing course time and time again. "This is worse than a gymkhana," Bert muttered, cutting in and out between red and black markers. Toward the east, snow was obscuring the mountains, drifting down almost to the water. He throttled back a little more, careful not to miss a turn in the poor visibility.

"Funny we haven't seen any deer or bear along the shoreline," I said. "Thought this country was alive with such critters."

Bert didn't take his eyes off the twisting channel. "Oh, there's plenty. Just watch sharp around the fresh-water streams. It's too early for the deer and their fawns, but you might see a bear or two."

"How about seals . . . or sea lions?"

"No. Not in here. They live out in deep water and on islands where they can't get caught. They're smart. I know we'll see some up around Taku Inlet when we start fishing. There's whole colonies in that place, just waiting for us to get our nets out. You'll see."

He spun us around a particularly sharp turn, looking back to watch the stern. "Yes sir, those robbers will grab a fish and eat a little, then grab another. Can ruin your catch and you'll never know it until you start to reel in."

We made another zig-zag. Up ahead, Carl was rolling the *Patsy* into a series of smooth turns, cutting the boat gracefully and staying clear of each channel marker by a comfortable margin.

"There's plenty of moose up here too," continued Bert. "Why I remember one fall when old man Wilson shot a bull right off the boat."

Not knowing Mr. Wilson I was a trifle confused. "What was the moose doing on the boat?" I asked.

"There wasn't no moose ON his boat. There was a moose on shore and he shot it FROM his boat."

"Oh, I see."

"The old boy, Wilson, was fishing up above Scow Cove and there was an oil drum on the bank at the high tide mark, so he takes the skiff and goes ashore to see if it's full of gasoline. Sometimes they are, you know. Anyway, when he gets ashore there are some nice big moose tracks around the drum and he plans accordingly.

"The next day, real early in the morning, he comes drifting by and sure enough, a great big bull walks out of the woods. Well, he shot him right there. So the bull laid on the sand bar until the tide flooded, then he put a line on him and towed him clear down to the powerhouse. They got a hoist down there. They hoisted the moose right onto Wilson's deck and into town he came with him. Dressed him out on the way.

"Some sport was up here from the States, and he says he wants to buy the bull. Wilson says, 'Okay. It'll cost you a thousand dollars. Had to go clean up to the North Pole to get him. Brought him down by dog-sled.'

"Well, this sport was impressed. He sort of figured that the price was terrible, but you don't get a moose every day that's been shot at the North Pole, so he gives the old man a thousand—cash."

While I thought about Mr. Wilson and the thousand dollars, I noticed a definite thinning in the weather. "Going to bust out in a minute," I said. And we did. Near Mountain Point we slid through a gray curtain into clear going, although the wind continued cold.

"Boy, I'm glad that crud is behind us," Bert called to the *Patsy.* "I feel like we're really making progress now."

Faye answered. "Carl's down below, but I sure agree with you. How's everything going?"

Bert didn't answer. The spook was making strange sounds. "Damn funny," he muttered. "Can't figure why we are getting so much static." He stepped back and turned the volume down. The noise continued.

"What the hell?" he growled. Finally he stopped the engine. Immediately the strange sounds ceased.

Swearing resignedly, he peeled back the rug and opened the engine-compartment hatch. In the darkness he could see brownish foam, bubbling and dripping into the bilge. "Oh, crap. The damn fresh-water pump has let go."

He crawled down, fumbled the light on and looked at the mess. "It's the pump, that's for sure—and I just had it rebuilt. Well, that's that for now." He crawled back out and glanced toward shore. "Hey! Keep a sharp watch. We don't want to pile up on the rocks."

He called the *Patsy.* "Come on back, Carl. I've got to have a tow. See if you can get here before I have to put the hook out." He did not want to restart the engine but knew it would be necessary if the boat drifted in much farther.

Captain Nelson came booming back. He slid the *Patsy* alongside and we tied the boats together in a hurry. Then Carl opened his throttle. Slowly, we eased away from the rocky shore.

"Have a cup of coffee," said Faye, handing one to Bert. He nodded his appreciation. "You too?" she asked.

"Thanks, not now," I replied. "Just finished one of Bert's and my stomach is a little uneasy."

The old man muttered, "Well, I'm going to save some fuel today. I'll just use yours. Funny, I had that pump overhauled in

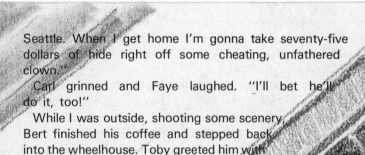

Seattle. When I get home I'm gonna take seventy-five dollars of hide right off some cheating, unfathered clown."

Carl grinned and Faye laughed. "I'll bet he'll do it, too!"

While I was outside, shooting some scenery, Bert finished his coffee and stepped back into the wheelhouse. Toby greeted him with a snarl. "What's gone wrong now?"

In the darkness he could see brownish foam, bubbling and dripping into the bilge.

asked the old man. It was chilly inside. He puzzled for a moment, then he remembered. "I believe the fire has gone out." He hadn't pumped up the fuel tank for three days.

Even though the sun was shining, the wind continued raw and penetrating. Bert finally got the stove started, while Toby shivered and burrowed down into an old afghan, waiting for the oil heater to do its thing.

At 10:30 we reached the Petersburg public floats. Bert untied the *Dolores,* started the engine and berthed her as quickly as possible. More foam bubbled into the bilge before he was able to cut the power.

"Well, Toby," he said, "looks like you'll have to wait a few more days to get to Juneau. I'm sorry, but there is nothing I can do about it."

Bert spent nearly an hour getting the pump off. He cursed. "Look at those impeller blades. Those crooks didn't overhaul this pump at all." The blades were pitted with corrosion and nicked in many places. He wiggled the shaft and scowled. It had definite side-play. "They sure never touched the main bearings either." Then he examined the case. "Just a damn coat of paint, and that's all. Wish I had that shop foreman here. I'd thread his family jewels onto the shaft and spin up the engine."

Still fuming, Bert stormed up the ramp and sloshed through two blocks of puddles, paying scant heed. Peaceful by nature, the old man is meaner than a barbed-wire fence when double-crossed. He pounded upstairs into the office of the Petersburg Cold Storage Company.

"Here's a phone number," he said to the startled girl. "Call it and charge it to me."

"Yes sir." She looked bewildered. "Do I know you?"

"Yeah . . . well, maybe you don't, but the boss does. I sell you my fish. Now call that Seattle number. I've got to straighten out one gent today, and I don't mean maybe!"

It is possible that a seismic shock recorded that day is now in the books as another Alaska trembler. It was actually Bert on the telephone. The result, on the other end, was an agreement to put a new pump on the first available airplane.

Then Bert went looking for the plant manager and found him in the supply room. Did they have a spare pump in case the new one was delayed in shipment? The answer was, "No, sorry." Bert said, "Well, that figures," and went splashing out onto Main Street. I was hard pressed to keep up.

We stopped at the Harbor Bar to say hello to the friendly bartender. As usual, Norman was grinning through his great beard and taking care of at least 50 customers. He waved at Bert and set a vodka-and-tonic in front of him without being asked.

"You've got a good memory," said the old man.

The bearded one continued to grin. "I never forget what a customer likes."

"Yeah, but I ain't seen you for a year, at least."

"Oh? Has it been a year? Guess we sort of lose track of time up here. Anyway, that IS what you were going to order, isn't it?"

"Sure as hell is," said Bert.

Looking over at me, Norm said, "What's your poison?"

"If you don't have any sarsaparilla, I'll take the same as my father."

He glanced at Bert. "Is this your son?"

The old man was embarrassed. "Well, yes, but we don't want it advertised. He's a good boy all right, but not too bright. Go ahead, Norm, give him a drink. It will be legal, I guess."

"That's funny," said the bartender. "He looks reasonably intelligent. Was this one of your better attempts?"

We had two drinks, then wandered out and found some liver for Toby. Remembering an earlier brush with an unfriendly game warden, Bert stopped and bought a sport fishing license. No use taking chances. He might want to wet a line as well as the net.

The weather front we had penetrated earlier caught up with us midway to the boat. Situation normal. We were soaked by the time we got the door open.

Three airline flights came in the next day. Three times Bert went up the ramp and visited the office. Three times he drew a blank.

Carl came by on the morning of the second day. "I think I'll get going. No point in my hanging around. I'll just go up to the Harbor and get my nets strung, then when you get in, I'll help you."

"Sure, why not. If the pump doesn't show by tomorrow I won't make opening day anyway. There's no point in both of us missing out. No, go ahead. I'll be there when I get there."

"You'd better," said Carl. "Remember, it's my turn to cut the first king this year."

"Your son?" said the bartender. "That's funny, he looks reasonably intelligent."

"You don't think I'd forgotten, do you?"

"No way. Not you. Okay, buddy, I'll plan on seeing you by Saturday night."

Bert said, "Don't forget, get a dozen crabs cooked for Toby. He's been raising hob all day, just waiting for some."

Friday dawned wet and cold and genuinely miserable. Bert stayed in the sack until nearly plane time. "No point in getting up," he assured me. Anyway, he was enjoying a nagging headache and his mouth tasted poorly, "Like the Russian army bivouacked there," he explained. "They must be pushing bad ice at the Harbor Bar."

The cat was not sympathetic. He used his sandbox early, then started prowling, hoping to find an open window.

"Cut out that stomping around!" yelled Bert.

The first plane came in on schedule. "Nothing," reported the airport manager. We were both getting furious.

I wandered in to chat with Tom Thompson, the company vice-president, explaining that I was writing a book about the Alaskan fishing industry. "Haven't you got some Perkins diesels in your work boats?" I asked.

"We sure do," said Tom.

"Well, is there any reason why you couldn't loan us a water pump? We've got a brand new one coming—sometime. You could put that back on the same boat."

Mr. Thompson thought for a minute. "I think that would be all right." Then turning to Bert, who had wandered in, "The boss is down south but I know he'd go along with it. I'll call the plant manager and tell him to fix you up."

So it came to pass that Bert found himself involved in sort of a Chinese fire drill, all quite innocently. I had gone exploring Petersburg, so only got the story second-hand.

The manager assigned a machinist to remove the fresh-water circulating pump from a company work boat. In the process, a gasket was ruined. Bert went out to buy some gasket material. Then the girl in the office found him by making many phone calls. It seemed that a package *HAD* arrived after all, and at that moment was being brought to town in a company automobile.

"Oh ho," said Bert happily, returning several pieces of gasket material, much to the disgust of the clerk. The old man hurried to the plant and told the manager that he wouldn't need the pump after all. That worthy gentleman said, "Gosh, Bert, that's fine—but where's the gasket? Gotta have one when we put the pump back on the boat."

So Bert hurried out to the marine supply store and said, "I'll need that material after all." It didn't go over too well because the clerk had shoved it back in stock and couldn't find it right away.

Bert picked up the box containing the pump and headed for the *Dolores.* "Now, by damn, we'll get under way!"

Walking down the long ramp, it dawned on him that the box was far too heavy to contain a lightweight pump for the Perkins. He stopped in the rain and opened it . . . and cried just a little. It was a pump all right, with a nice big brass armature, used exclusively on an electrically driven Worthington.

Slowly he walked back to the office. He told the girl of his troubles. He also told Mr. Thompson. Mr. Thompson called the plant manager and instructed him to remove the pump again. And Bert got on the phone and had another unfriendly chat with some guy in Seattle.

They nearly had the pump off when the nice girl from the front office came rushing down the stairs and found the old man in the machine shop, cutting a gasket.

"They made a little mistake at the airport," she reported gaily. "The gentleman waiting for a Worthington pump . . . well, he got yours, and he's calling Seattle and I couldn't listen to such language, so I thought I'd come down and tell you."

"You're a good girl," said Bert. "Now, will you do me a favor? Please tell the plant manager that I don't need his pump after all. Frankly, I don't DARE tell him!"

He installed the new pump and it worked like a charm.

Then he tried to tidy up the bilge. *That* pump refused to do its job and pretty soon he found that the link-belt was slipping. So he walked back up town.

The fellow in the marine supply store looked at him suspiciously. "You SURE you want this belting? Remember, I've got to cut it."

"Yes," said Bert apologetically. "Cut her 52-inches long. I promise not to bring it back."

He stopped and bought a can of shrimp for Toby. Next he stopped at the Harbor Bar and found me sitting there, trying to get warm. "The only thing between this town and the North Pole is a screen door," I assured him.

He considered the remark carefully. "You know," he said soberly, "you are totally spoiled. Why, I've seen it so cold up here that thermometers busted and boiling water would freeze right on the stove. Sure, there's a little chill in the air, but that's good for you. Puts the old spring in your step."

"I'm going to sit here and thaw out," I retorted.

After a while he said, "Let's go get us a salmon steak and then fix that poor old engine."

We were in the heart of the salmon country, so getting a salmon steak at a restaurant would seem to be a simple matter. However, Bert demanded to see the fish before it was cooked.

The waitress said, "No."

The manageress said, "No."

The cook came out, looked our way and shook his head.

Bert said, quite loudly, "I want to see that fish. You wouldn't buy a pair of shoes without trying them on—or a pair of pants—or a new coat. And I ain't going to eat your fish unless I *see* it!"

The cook went into the kitchen and returned with two slabs of tired-looking fish on a plate.

"What in hell is that?" Bert asked.

"It's fresh salmon."

"Fresh my neck. Not only that but you've sliced it off behind the tail. There ain't enough meat there to feed a sick cat. Now go get us two slices that are fit to eat!"

I expected a fight, right then and there, but it didn't happen. The cook just looked at him, went slam-banging into the kitchen and never came back.

So we had ham and eggs. Not that the meal was good, but at least it was filling. It ought to be, at nearly four bucks apiece.

"Too many tourists up here," said Bert. "But they shouldn't try to sell the stern of a dogfish to an old gill-netter like me."

Chapter Eleven

PETERSBURG—TAKU HARBOR

With all pumps and belts operating properly and the old Perkins chuffing smoothly, we eased out of Petersburg at four o'clock in the morning. We cut inside the Sukoi Island, skirted Beacon Point and headed for Cape Strait light. The sky and sea were both gray but the glass was up to 30:08.

"This is going to be a fine day," said the old man.

Angling across Frederick Sound, an easterly breeze began to shove us along nicely. "Quite a change," I said.

Bert nodded and took a generous pinch of snuff. He checked our speed at Cape Fanshaw. "By golly," he chuckled, "we're making eight knots. Not too shabby for this old girl."

Shortly thereafter I nearly wrecked the whole expedition. Bird Rock was ahead, with Storm Island laying to the north, and between the two the chart indicated real shoal water, full of hidden reefs. Anyone with a modicum of sense would have checked the chart and stayed clear of such a spot. Even a junior Sea Scout would have known that the Bird Rock marker spelled disaster unless kept to starboard. So I blithely kept it to port.

"Hey, Bert," I called. "Come up and see the birds flying across the bow. Must be a million gulls or terns up ahead." Both sky and water looked white as countless waterfowl moved from Fanshaw Bay toward Bird Rock.

It's very seldom that the old man really swears. True, his language is quite salty, but for once he really let go with some jim-dandy cuss words. Simultaneously he yanked the throttle back and crammed the drive into reverse.

After the paint quit blistering on the wheelhouse walls, we got the *Dolores* turned around and felt our way out of the rock pile—and none too soon, either. With an ebb tide, new shoals and reefs kept popping up on all sides. It was not a reassuring sight.

"Well, now that we've had today's lesson in navigation, I'm going to cook breakfast," said Bert. "How do you want your eggs?"

"Dipped in hemlock," I replied.

Fortunately we had both taken advantage of our forced delay in Petersburg and caught up with many on-board chores, including dishwashing. "Nice to have a clean plate," Bert observed.

We let the auto-pilot clank and wheeze during breakfast and passed The Five Fingers while sipping coffee. "The only way to go," said Bert. "We just don't get weather like this very often. Somebody must be living right."

Nearing the checkpoint abeam Point Hobart, the old man began to watch for more of his porpoise friends. "They should be out here someplace," he told me. "I'm going to try for some pictures. Did I tell you I bought film in Petersburg?"

"Hey, here they come," he yelled a few minutes later. Toby jumped through the port window and scuttled for the foredeck. Bert hurried out after him, leaving me to hold a steady course. He waved to his friends and started snapping furiously. "Wish you'd slow down," he cried. "You're jumping too fast."

For those who have never tried to catch the smooth movements of porpoise, it is suggested that a movie camera is far more suitable than a single-frame instrument. The beauties dash about with unbelievable grace, but fast. Certainly Bert photographed more splashes than porpoises. Finally I kicked in the auto-pilot and took a turn also.

As rapidly as they had appeared, they gave one last leap and dived out of sight. The old man went inside chuckling. "Hope I caught one or two."

Toward noon the *Wickersham* came down Stephens Passage. She was a good two miles to port, loaded to the hilt with early season tourists. "Bet they're having a beautiful trip, eh Toby?" said Bert. "You and I should try that some time."

"I suppose everybody will see our porpoise friends today," he added.

After a while he said, "We'll be getting up by Tracy Arm in an hour or so. Think I'll see if there's any bergs floating around. We could use some good ice. Not like that treated, half-frozen stuff you get in town."

Throttling back, we eased close to shore near Point Coke. Small icebergs were drifting out of Holkham Bay, moving sedately with the tide. Some were grounded in shallow water while others sailed on into Stephens Passage. They all glittered in the sun, translucent blue-green. Beautiful to see, but deadly.

"Guess you know that about 90 percent of these babies is out of sight," said the old man. "There's more ice below the surface than you can imagine. Sometimes they take weeks to melt."

"Well, don't make like the *Titanic*," I replied.

"Oh, no sweat. Look right over there. See that small piece floating all by itself?"

"Yeah."

"Well, that's for us." He swung the boat around and chopped the throttle. "Now, here's enough fresh ice to last a week. Guess I'll get some for Carl, too. He said there wasn't any out here when they came by."

He started breaking the ice into smaller pieces, whacking it with a long-handled gaff. "The Iceman Cometh!" he yelled.

The landing net proved to be handy. Working rapidly, he soon had a good supply piled on deck. "Okay," he said. "Now, we'll skirt inside Midway Island and head for home. How's that suit you, Toby?"

My personal experience with Midway Island had been confined to careless gooney birds being sucked into jet engines, to the detriment of all concerned. Therefore I took a fast look at the chart to make sure we weren't in mid-Pacific.

No, this Midway was on the east side of Stephens Pass.

We were off Point Styleman when a whale surfaced dead ahead. The black body appeared far larger than the little boat, which it was. "Whoops!" said Bert explosively.

Toby jumped up to the forward window just as the huge mammal stuck its head down and dived. With horror, the cat saw the tail, far wider than the wheelhouse, rise majestically, then disappear into the oily sea. With a wild howl, he jumped for his refuge in the head.

The old man laughed. "Take over, will you?" He went aft for some ice, then quite methodically built a pair of long, cool drinks. "Here's to the million-year ice," he said.

He was right. Icebergs in these waters come from nearby glaciers. The million-year-old estimate may be grossly minimal. Many scientists believe the remains of the ice-cap to be several million years old. The ice is clear as crystal. Formed by nature long before man cluttered the world with pollutants, the transparent material refuses to melt like the modern variety. There are no

"The Ice-Man cometh," yelled Bert.

impurities to either trap or hold heat. Bert took another sip. "Now, *THAT'S* a drink!"

We poked along for another hour, finally passing Port Snettisham. To the southwest we could see the snow-covered mountains on Glass Peninsula. The sea remained calm, the sky uncluttered.

"More like August than April," said Bert. "As a matter of fact, it's *TOO* damn nice. I'm sort of afraid of what Sunday will bring. Probably bounce us all over the whole inlet."

As we approached Stockade Point, Toby shot outside. He ran to the bow and watched as our little boat moved into the quiet harbor. Then as we turned to starboard, he could see the float and the shed. And he could see the *Patsy* and the *Lituya.* Further in he could see the cabins. He must have been thinking happily, "Oh boy, I'm home at last."

While we were getting tied to the float, Toby made one wild jump and hit running. He dashed up to Vern and Coral and Carl and Faye, greeting each in turn.

"Hey look, Toby," said Vern. "Got a whole bucket of crabs. Cooked 'em just for you!"

Yes indeed, it was nice to get back home.

The evening was quite memorable, to me anyway. I feared at first that I would be like an illegitimate son at a family reunion, but that certainly was not the case. Vern and Coral Dick welcomed me like a member of the clan, and Tiger Olson came puttering up in his little kicker, waving a jug of "welcome-home" juice.

"Tell you what," boomed Bert, "let's all have a drink and then I've got to get my net ready. Can't wait until tomorrow."

Carl said, "That's the way I see it, too. I've got everything all set. Let's swing your stern around to the float and get that reel loaded. We've still got a good three hours of daylight."

Not knowing anything about rigging nets, I did the smartest thing possible—stayed out of the way. Tiger and I sat on the float, watching the operation and sipped our dinner.

"Suppose I should help 'em," observed the Tiger. "Ain't goin' to, though. When you get to be 92, you've done all the work required of one man."

"Amen," I said. "You sure don't look 92."

"Well, I am. Got a family Bible to prove it. Spent most of my life up here, too. See that hill over there?" pointing.

"Yes."

"Solid pyrite. All mine. Worth about 10 million or so—but I can't get nobody to buy it, yet. You know what pyrite is, don't you?"

"I'm not too sure," I replied honestly.

"Okay, I'll tell you. Pyrite is really iron disulfide. They burn the stuff to make sulfur dioxide and sulfuric acid. And the whole mountain is solid with it. I found it and filed a claim, all legal and proper. She's mine."

"Just like having money in the bank," I commented.

"Well, not really," he said. "I made a mistake last year. I was up in Juneau talking with this Japanese fellow, trying to interest them in mining, and I says she's worth ten million dollars if she's worth a cent.

"So we talked a while and had a few drinks, then I seen a guy listening to us, real close. And I remembered I'd seen him someplace.

"Well sir, my state pension check didn't come the next time nor the next, so I went up to see 'em about it. Sure enough, it was the same guy in the office I'd seen in the bar.

"He wasn't very sociable, either. Said that anybody with ten million dollars was swindling the state by accepting a monthly check.

"That made me so damn mad I went right over to see the governor. *He* knows I ain't sold the mountain, so he gets on the phone and has a few words with the guy who held out on me, and I've been gettin' my checks ever since.

"Now, I know the hill is worth plenty, but I can't dig up pyrite and eat it."

I agreed. We had another cup and the old sourdough got started all over again.

"Had a bad spell last fall," he said. "The doctor didn't know what it was. Thought maybe I'd eaten some spoiled food, but of course I hadn't.

"Anyway, he could see I was failing fast, so he had me fly down to Seattle. Packed in like a sardine on that airline plane. Must have been 200 people on her. And rough! We bounced all over the sky. In and out of clouds. That feller drivin' her was good, though. Never hit nothin'.

"So we got to Seattle and I told 'em I had to go to the hospital and they was real worried because I didn't know which one.

"Hey look, Toby. Got a whole bucket of crabs. Cooked 'em just for you!"

Guess there's a half-dozen down there. So the airline man called Juneau and gets my doctor and he tells him that I'm supposed to go to a Virgin-Something-or-other, I forget now, and that's where they sent me. Cost over five dollars to get there.

"Boy, I never seen so many automobiles. It ain't safe, I can tell you for sure. And the taxicab feller must have thought I was dying 'cause he sure hurried. I was afraid to look out, so I laid down on the seat and shut my eyes. Then he *REALLY* speeded her up.

"Well, I got to the hospital and they put me in a bed and made me take a bath and hid my clothes and wouldn't let me smoke or have a drink and pulled some bedsheets around me, so I couldn't see nobody.

"Pretty soon old Doc Herman comes to the door and looks in. He tells the nurse to move me to ISOLATION. 'He's got the Satanic flu,' says the doctor.

"Sure'n hell it's the Satanic flu. You never heard of it? Well, once there was the London flu, then the Hong Kong flu and the Asiatic flu, and I guess the South American flu, and the people that lived there didn't want no disease named for them. So the doctors thought about it, and finally said it was all alike and decided to call it Satanic. Named it for the Old Harry himself.

"Then they found out I had been with all kinds of people. Boy-oh-boy, did that upset 'em!

"Doc Herman called all the other doctors in Seattle and told 'em I had the Satanic flu and that they'd be lucky if there wasn't an epidemic. They thought maybe 50- or 60-thousand people would die. Had 'em really worried, I can tell you.

"Well, I got over it and came home. Sure cost a pile of money and I guess a lot of people DID get the disease. That's why I wanted to get out of Seattle. Didn't want to catch it again.

"Now . . . I think we'd better have a drink. It's the ONLY thing I know of to keep the bugs offn' a feller."

Chapter Twelve

THE KINGS DONE COME

A thin overcast blanked off the morning sun, keeping Taku Harbor dark and chilly. A coating of frost made for treacherous walking on the floats and along the deck.

"Watch your step," warned Vern as I came out of the warm wheelhouse.

I paused, waiting to catch my breath in the cold air. "This is the day, hey Vern? What's your hunch—are we going to get a boatload?"

"Of course. With Uncle Bert to guide us, what else?"

Bert came out, shivering. "Boy, it's colder than a well-digger's rear end. Thought you said spring had come, Vern."

"No, I said I was glad winter was over. Didn't say anything about spring. Anyway, this year summer will be here before spring."

"By golly, I believe you." Then to me, "Ready to go after the big ones?"

"I'm ready. Now, before we head out, what do you want me to do today?"

He smiled. "Toby and I will handle everything this trip. You just watch and make notes and keep the coffee pot full. Anyway, there isn't room for two people back in the well, so don't worry about trying to help."

Vern said, "If you guys are ready, let's go get 'em."

Bert chuckled. "Oh, I'm ready all right but we can't set until noon. Might as well have another cup of coffee. It's going to be damn cold up in the inlet. I can smell it."

The women came out, looked at the gray sky, commented briefly about the idiocy of fishing and ducked back inside.

I realized there was intense suppressed excitement in the air. These people were truly spring-loaded, all of them.

Bert went inside and fired up the old Perkins. It rumbled smoothly. The *Lituya* came to life, belching blue smoke. Carl looked at me and waved. "Tell Bert 'Good fishing.'" He hopped onto the *Patsy*. A moment later it started its quiet rumble too. We were ready for the kings.

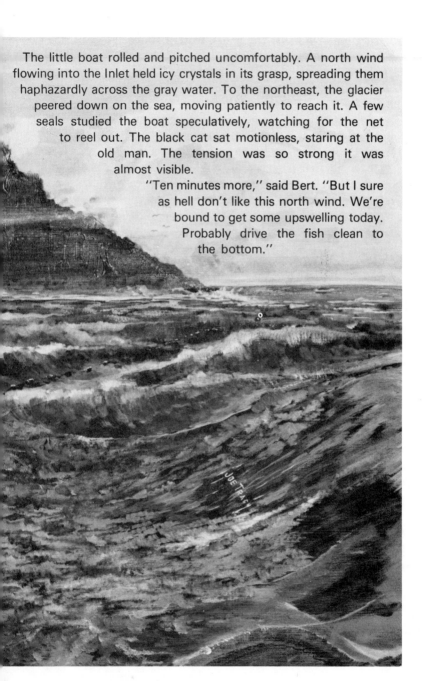

The little boat rolled and pitched uncomfortably. A north wind flowing into the Inlet held icy crystals in its grasp, spreading them haphazardly across the gray water. To the northeast, the glacier peered down on the sea, moving patiently to reach it. A few seals studied the boat speculatively, watching for the net to reel out. The black cat sat motionless, staring at the old man. The tension was so strong it was almost visible.

"Ten minutes more," said Bert. "But I sure as hell don't like this north wind. We're bound to get some upswelling today. Probably drive the fish clean to the bottom."

We were ready for the kings.

The rain had started. The spook blatted above the cat's head, causing him to twitch slightly. "Hey, *Dolores S,*" said a faint voice. "You there, Bert?"

The old man unhooked the microphone, squeezing the button. "Yeah, you bet," he yelled. "Right here, Carl, just about ready to give 'em hell!" The boat pitched up and over a long roller, pounding into the uneasy water. "How about you? Where are you now?" Instinctively he braced himself while waiting for a reply.

"Oh, we're up here near Jaw Point. I don't think it's much good though. There's trash all over the place, lots of it. But, I guess we'll try anyway."

"Yeah. Good fishing to you." He hung up the mike and squinted across the inlet. Finally he picked up his ancient binoculars and studied the opposite shore. He spotted the little double-ender, almost hidden by the point, and wondered why they had picked that spot. "Maybe he knows something I don't know," he said. "Anyway, this is as good a place as any." He paused and looked at the battered clock. "Hell, let's get it out. It's that time."

Almost automatically, Bert got into his work gear: rubber boots, yellow oilskins, waist-length rubber coat and the old so'wester. The new orange gloves went on hard. He fought them silently. Then he was ready. I stepped out onto the aft deck to watch. Immediately I shivered.

The first blast of rain-filled air caused him to gasp. "Should have waited another month." Getting down into the well, he worked the red marker buoy loose and dumped it overboard, then methodically started unreeling the 900 feet of net, the corks bumping and thumping as they pitched over the stern roller.

He watched the net and his course simultaneously. Twice he altered course, using the aft wheel, letting the boat crawl forward slowly. Directly in back, sheer rock cliffs, decorated with evergreens and patchy snow, rose into the overcast sky. A few gulls moved in to observe the operation. They hung motionless, balanced in the north wind, and talked quietly among themselves.

He continued to pay out the net until 150 fathoms of white and red corks lay on the water, turning and twisting like a multi-colored snake. Satisfied, he stopped the reel and set the brake.

At six minutes past noon, he popped back into the warm wheelhouse. His rain-soaked glasses steamed over instantly. He fumbled for a tissue, wiping his nose and then the glasses, noting little improvement in the condition of either. Finally he got out of the rubber gear and hung it to drip.

Toby looked up as if to say, "There must be a better way to make a living."

Bert looked at the old cat and grinned. "Cheer up. You'll have a king liver for supper tonight."

Thus the first set of the season was made. Bert took a pinch of snuff, settled down by the starboard window and picked up a copy of *Playboy.* Just beyond the boat a seal stuck its head out and looked at the *Dolores* with big sad eyes.

Seals and sea lions are smart indeed. They know when a free meal is in the offing. Why chase after your food when good old *homo sapiens* will bring it right to your door? Still, one has to be careful. Some of those men are downright sneaky, like shooting at you or dropping explosive "salutes" right in your face. Best to sit off at a discreet distance and keep a wary eye out for any overt movement on board.

Some days it's a long wait. Today was one. The corks floated high with little movement except to follow the constant undulations of the water. No threshing or boiling to indicate a customer.

"Damn corks are gonna get sunburned," grumbled the old man, spitting overboard. He closed the sliding window against the driving rain and resumed reading.

At 3:30 p.m. the first action began. Two sections of corks were working and a third looked promising. Bert groaned a little as he struggled into the foul-weather gear.

Two-hundred-and-fifty feet of net came in before the first fish showed, entangled in the net. "One down," Bert said, and laughed. "The kings done come."

He jabbed the struggling salmon with a short-handled gaff and rolled it into the well. He stopped the reel and struck the fish twice, two sharp blows just behind the eyes. Immediately it ceased to struggle.

With the skill known to gill-netters, Bert untangled the fish and shoved it aside. Then he straightened the net and started the reel again, deftly separating the cork line, the net and the lead line. He fed the net onto the roller, building a constant level, much as an automatic take-up fills the sport fisherman's reel.

Two more kings came aboard. Each time he repeated the process while the raw rain continued to stream down his face, blurring his vision.

When the red buoy whumped against the stern, Bert dragged it aboard and eased the throttle to half-speed. He spun the little steering wheel hard to port, and jockeying the boat carefully, eased back toward the original set area, watching for landmarks along the precipitous shoreline.

He reset the net, the little boat bouncing more as the tide turned, and shivered as a cupful of icy water found a channel under the old rain hat. Toby, who had come to supervise, made a sure-footed dash back through the open starboard window.

Bert came inside shivering, and shucked off the rubber gear. "By damn, it's miserably cold. Wonder where the sun is. It must be over the yardarm by now."

"It is," I said, handing him a drink. "I sort of figured you could stand a little medicine."

"Bless you," he said simply.

About 5:30 he said to Toby, "Well, you old black bum, guess I'd better clean the fish if you're going to have dinner."

Bert went aft and cleaned the three big kings. He put the gutting board in place, kicked on the hose and opened the fish quickly. Two cuts took care of the breathing apparatus behind the gills. One slash laid the belly open from anus to chin. The entrails were pulled loose and the two red strips of roe separated and laid aside. Next the livers were removed and saved for the Second-In-Command. Opening the holding bin, he dumped the three big fish in quite unceremoniously. It had taken him less than five minutes.

Standing the gutting board on end, Bert blasted it clean with a stream of sea water. The self-bailing well was washed until scrupulously tidy. Finally he hosed his rubber clothing thoroughly. Satisfied, he cut off the salt-water pump. "This boat never smelled fishy and it ain't going to start now," he said. "I hose her down good as soon as the fish are clean."

He placed the six strips of roe in a plastic bag and tied the neck carefully. Then, almost religiously, he cut the liver into bite-size pieces and placed a small pile on the aft deck. Even before he was done, Toby shot out of the house and dove into the fresh food.

At 6:30 p.m., two more fine kings came aboard. Bert was almost ready to set again when I told him the *Patsy* was calling. He came in, cold and dripping, and grabbed the microphone. "Hello Captain Carl. What's on your mind?"

"I'm still working here, off the point. If you guys want your supper, come on over."

"Okay. What have you done, cut a king for us?"

"Yeah. Had to. Seal got at a beauty, so we might as well eat that one. I've cut a piece for you and I'm saving some for the *Lituya* as soon as I can raise Vern. He's up near Troller's Anchorage, I think. Anyway, we're blocked off. Maybe you can read him. I know I can't."

"Yeah," bellowed the old man. "I'll give it a try."

Vern came back immediately. "Hey, Captain Bert, sounds like you were talking with the *Patsy*. What's up?"

"Got your supper. Carl's down below Jaw Point. Says to come on over and get a slice of king. I'm going on across now. I'll see you there."

"Okay, okay. Will do. See you there. Over."

Within 15 minutes the three little boats converged. Even before the *Dolores* was secured to the *Patsy*, Toby leaped several feet across open water, landing on the deck with a substantial thump. Faye hollered at him, "Come on in, you old so-and-so. Got some liver for you."

Toby looked at the woman and shook his head. He was already stuffed. He felt it was his duty, though, to explore the boat. Then, as he glanced to port, another boat slid in quietly. TWO vessels to inspect simultaneously. Might as well get on with it. He leaped nimbly aboard the *Lituya*.

Coral met him at the wheelhouse door. "Hey, come on in, Toby. I've saved you some crab meat. Thought you might be visiting today."

Stuffed or not, he couldn't resist a dish of fresh Dungeness crab. It would be an effort, but he elected to give it a try.

"Maybe we should have a drink," suggested Bert.

"Not me," said Carl. "Like I told you this morning, I was up most of last night and near all of today. Cramps. Think I'd better go in early tomorrow and check with the Marine Hospital."

"He sure as hell will," Faye declared, "I don't like his color one bit and he's doing more than having cramps."

Vern and Bert and I had a drink while the two wives chatted. We didn't linger long. The late Alaskan sun was dropping behind the hills and the sea had flattened.

"Better get back and set again," said Bert. "Got to fill the lanterns before dark." Soon the boats separated, each going its own way.

Reaching his selected spot, Bert placed a kerosene lantern on a rubber inner tube float and attached it to the net. It replaced the red marker buoy. Carefully, he eased the light onto the water, then picked up a heading of 90 degrees and started toward the Scar, unreeling the net at slow speed.

At 9:10 p.m. the set was completed. With the wind now little more than a whisper and a perfectly flat sea, the night promised to be comfortable. To the north we could see three tiny spots of light.

"Maybe I can welcome the fish before they do," he said as Toby came out to check the set. "And now let's cook us a few slabs of salmon."

We drifted through the night, the long net acting as a sea anchor, keeping the *Dolores* on a southeasterly heading and away from the rocky shore. Bert checked the set twice during the hours of darkness. Apparently the salmon were sleeping and it wasn't until six o'clock that action started. By then the wind had picked up and the sea was fussing around a little. One fat king came in, flopping helplessly. "Good start," said the old man.

At 10 a.m. two young fellows from the Fish and Game Department came bouncing alongside in a small outboard. They were friendly but a trifle officious. Sorry, but they had to see the ship's papers and Bert's license.

Bert had expected them. Patiently he went through the routine. He winked at me when one youngster asked, "How many in the crew?"

"Two," said Bert. "I'm the Master. Toby here is Second-in-Command."

The young man looked at me. "What's your status on this boat?"

"I'm just riding."

"Oh, come on, you've got to be doing something."

"Nope. Just riding."

"Now wait a minute. I think you're fishing and if you are, I'm going to see your license."

"I'm not fishing."

"If you're not fishing, what are you doing on a fishing boat?"

"Bartending and writing a book."

He scowled. "I'd better see your identification."

"Okay," I said, holding out my military ID.

The kid looked embarrassed. "Gee, I'm sorry, SIR."

"Not long out of the service yourself, are you?"

"No, SIR."

They went back to their launch and took off toward Cooper Point.

"I can't see any sense in all that," I told Bert. "If the sovereign state thinks you are fishing illegally, can't they just wait until you go in to unload and then grab you? Why disturb fishermen when their nets are out?"

Bert shrugged. "True, but you can't buck city hall."

At two minutes before noon, Bert had the net in and secured. Twelve nice king salmon lay in the fish box. "Not too good," said the old man, "but the safest way to start the season. Everybody knows it's bad luck to begin with a big haul." He looked at Toby, "Ready to go home?"

The cat appeared to nod. His homing instincts told him Juneau was just around the corner. Bert's wife Kit and an Indian boy had found him there 12 years earlier, in a garbage can. He was the only kitten still alive, out of six in the can. Kit had brought him to the *Dolores* and somehow managed to save his life. So Juneau was really home and he was about to return for the first time since the previous September.

Chapter Thirteen

A TOURIST LOOKS AT JUNEAU

I had been looking forward to this trip with considerable enthusiasm. I read everything I could find about Alaska, and some of the public relations handouts intrigued me no end. One brochure declared that I would see some majestic scenery, "forested slopes that rise straight from the clean, unpolluted sea, often backed by snow-capped peaks while hundreds of dark, lonely islands speckle the ice-blue waters."

Another pitch that got me right over the old squadron-patch was a statement that perhaps I would see many seals sunning themselves on ice floes, illuminated by long hours of summer sun. As for shopping, I was promised things my bride and I simply couldn't do without—whales' teeth, candied jellyfish flukes, Indian silverwork and hand-carved Eskimo ivory.

I did see seals, lots of them, but not a solitary one on an ice floe. Personally, I think they have better sense than to float around on floes. I'm sure that I wouldn't want to do that and I'm certain that they must know better.

Perhaps I enjoyed one distinct advantage over the average tourist. I was already hardened to life in Alaska, even before we arrived for our first real shore leave. Certainly no tourist ship or scheduled airline can boast of food comparable with Bert's stew or my burned eggs. Those are things that must be experienced if one is to appreciate them fully. Then too, because of a paucity of fresh water, we had refrained from bathing for about 15 days. That also did a great deal to condition me, physically and mentally, for my introduction to life in the Alaska Panhandle. Even Toby sat as far away from us as possible.

Our initial contact with Juneau started at the Juneau Cold Storage Company. We pulled in at their dock and unloaded the modest haul of king salmon, a total of 12. "Not too good," said Bert, "but at a dollar a pound, guess we can't kick." The dozen weighed in at 288 pounds.

After hosing out the fish box, we cranked up, headed under the Juneau-Douglas bridge and cut into Boat Harbor. There we found a berth of sorts, a temporary haven from the elements. We tied beside a rather sickly-looking troller. I suspected it might sink at any moment, particularly when we crossed her aft deck and I could see oily water bubbling up in the open bilge. "Oh, this is just fine," said the old man happily.

We took a change of underwear and socks ashore. "We'll go down to the company office and get our mail and then have a drink. How's that sound?" Bert is the eternal optimist.

"If it's all the same to you," I replied, "I'd like to find a hotel and get scrubbed down before we mix with too many people. Might drive them completely away."

We hit the jackpot on mail. There was a tape for Bert from Annie that pleased him immensely, and some bills that pleased him not one whit. I found a letter from my bride and that made my day complete.

"Now," said Bert, "I think we should walk over to the Sailor's Sauna and get some of the fish and dirt cooked out of our hides."

"Sauna!" I said. "I want an honest-to-goodness hot shower, with lots of soap. I'm afraid a steambath would just set the stink."

He laughed. "It's not really a sauna. An old gal takes your money and gives you towels and soap and shows you to a shower room."

"Well, that's some better," I said. "No hotel?"

"No hotel. Wait a minute, let's go in here for a quickie."

The place turned out to be the New York Tavern, and the joint was jumping. An Indian gal of indeterminate age saw the old man coming through the swinging doors. She jumped up and rushed to meet him, her face aglow with complete delight.

"Hey Bert, you old -----------!" she yelled, flying into his arms. He hugged her and grinned. In the ensuing hubbub, I couldn't hear his reply. His expression was enough. He was home!

We met at least a score of old friends and I not only shook hands with one and all, but also had to accept an endless supply of drinks. You don't say "no thanks" to any friend of Bert's. By and by I lost track of time and didn't really care whether I got a bath or not, but somehow we arrived at the Sailor's Sauna, just how I'm not at all certain. The place was so crowded Bert and I had to share the same shower, and that helped bring me back to reality. The old man suddenly turned the shower up full blast to

The old man suddenly turned the shower up full blast to cold. Of course he thought it was funny while I was trying to get my breath.

cold. Of course he thought it was funny while I was trying to get my breath.

As we dressed I asked, "How much for the shower?"

"A dollar-fifty-five each," he said. "I paid the old girl before she'd let us in. Now isn't this better than a $20 hotel?"

"Saved about 17 bucks," I said, trying to do arithmetic in a fuzzy headbone.

"You bet," he bellowed. "We can eat and have a couple drinks on the money we saved."

Bert ordered black cod at the friendly, waterfront restaurant. "Don't you ever get tired of fish?" I asked.

"No," he replied. "What are you having?"

"Liver and onions and spuds," I answered.

It didn't take long for me to realize why he had ordered fish. At least it was fresh. My portion of liver certainly had flavor, but not a flavor I could recognize. The slightly warmed raw onions and the sour potatoes didn't do much for me either.

"Yes sir," said Bert, wiping his mouth, "fish is the safest thing you can get up here. What's the matter, ain't your liver no good?"

"It's delicious," I lied.

He looked at me closely, and at my virtually untouched plate. "Maybe we should get us a drink," he said finally. "You look like you could use one."

We went across the street to the jumping bar and made a phone call for transportation. It developed that there would be a slight delay before we could get a cab. "Going to have to wait," said the old man happily. "Let's sit down and have a drink with Ole, I see he's still here. You met him before dinner."

I remembered vaguely that I had shared a cup of cheer with the gentleman. So while we waited for a taxi we joined Ole again, and he was delighted.

Going back to the boat, the old man said, "I sure like that fellow. Did I ever tell you about my getting him a king?"

"No, I don't think so."

"Well, I ran into him in the Old Victory bar one afternoon and after we'd had a couple of drinks he says, 'Hey, how about bringing me a nice king next time you're out?' and of course I say's I'll do it. I'd only known him for 50 years, what else could I say?

"Anyway, when I come in I gave him a good big one, and naturally I wouldn't let him pay for it. That was a mistake. Now, every time I see him, he always buys the drinks and wants to thank me for that damn fish—and this is a good 10-12 years later.

"Last year I was hurrying by the bowling alley and out comes Ole, running after me. 'Come on back,' he says, 'and we'll have a drink.' I had a lot of business to complete that day, but I never got out of the bowling alley bar. I'll bet you he must have paid close to $100, maybe $200 for that fish."

By the time we got aboard, I was really sleepy. However, I was not destined for the sack because an old friend, whom I shall call General Grant, came staggering onto the *Dolores,* clutching a jug in each hand.

"By damn, it's the General," Bert announced. "Come on in and meet a buddy of mine," he bellowed.

I wasn't too sure I needed to meet anyone else that particular evening. I was done in, but reason prevailed. If the old man could keep going, I would make a valiant attempt.

"I come bearing gifts," said the General owlishly. "My cup runneth over . . . and I'm going to . . . to . . . to do the same. May I use your head?"

After half an hour of idle chatter, Bert realized that his friend really had been waiting for his return from the lower 48, and now that Bert was back, they'd have to do some serious catching up. Fortunately, for me, the friendly inebriate had a brand new camper and nothing would do but that we go look at it and settle down to some serious drinking.

The old man glanced at me and I shook my head. He said, "Well okay, General, let's go see your camper. You and I will walk up to the dock. The cook here is going to bed."

That was one of the nicest things he'd ever done. They departed through the aft door and I dove for the fo'castle. Toby started to say something about drunken sots, but I was asleep before he finished. I remember saying something about Juneau being a fine little city . . . or maybe I just dreamed it.

Chapter Fourteen

BUSY AT THE HARBOR

Vern was splicing a sizeable chunk into his net when we got back to Taku Harbor. "Damn shark," he told me. "Made a pretty big hole in her."

I looked at his handiwork. "Must have been a monster to rip out that much."

"No," he said seriously. "Probably not real big, but there's one thing you learn early in this business. A fish has a wonderful sense of smell, and if I left even one spot where the shark had rubbed, a salmon wouldn't come near the net. He'd smell that shark and just take off, wide open. So you sort of guess how much the shark messed up, and go ahead and cut it out."

"I didn't know they smelled that bad," I said.

"Boy, do they ever! Maybe not to you and me but to a fish, the odor scares 'em. And don't let anybody tell you we don't have sharks up here."

Coral came bouncing out of the wheelhouse. "Hey," she said, "how about a cup of coffee? Got a stick if you need a little tonic."

"Now that's real nice," I said. "Yes, I'd like some coffee, but no stick. Not after Juneau last night. We drank the place dry."

She handed me a steaming mug. "I doubt that. We've tried a couple times but it just doesn't work. They can bring it in faster than you can drink it up."

Vern agreed. "Not only that, but the price is way too high for us. You can shoot a whole week's fishing before you begin to get a glow on."

Bert came out and surveyed the operation. Coral said, "You sure look good. S'matter, a dogfish bite you?"

The old man managed a feeble smile. "Sure as hell did. A great big one."

"You know," interrupted Vern, "as soon as Carl gets back, we'd better get the float off. We're going to have a real high tide this afternoon and I think we can work it free without too much trouble."

The float in question is owned jointly by the two, Bert having 50 percent and Carl the balance. Which end belongs to whom has never been clearly established. In any event, a small shack reposes on the stern (or maybe the bow) in which they store spare nets, corks, leads, buoys and a butane heater. The heater is used exclusively for cooking crabs for Toby, and the float is their home-away-from-home. Both the *Patsy* and the *Dolores* tie to it from early spring until the fall exodus.

One unwritten law is scrupulously observed: "No trash in Taku Harbor." The water is far too beautiful and unpolluted to profane with garbage. Perhaps the hippie population of Juneau's Boat Harbor should take note. They throw everything overboard. A lot of good folks live aboard their boats but every year there are more of the free-loading longhairs.

Juneau docks also suffer from dog defecation. The poor canines are chained there by the unwashed kooks who live the communal life at the harbor and are too stupid and lazy to clean the floats.

Back in the clean country, we mapped out a campaign to un-stick the "Bert-Carl" dock, and I was amazed at the ingenuity displayed by this group of happy people. A few highly touted engineers with whom I have worked could have learned a lot by observing the operation.

Vern went ashore before high tide and studied the situation. "You know," he said upon return, "we're going to have a problem. The big log on the starboard side has popped out. It's just laying there on the beach."

"Which end?" asked Bert, wondering if his or Carl's end would prove troublesome.

"The end with the shed," said Vern. "Don't you know port from starboard?"

"No," said Bert, "I don't unless I'm sure which is the bow and which is the stern."

"Well," replied Vern, "I've long suspected you didn't know your butt from a hole in the ground. Dammit, the log under *your* side of the shack is missing. Now, what do we do?"

Bert went inside and mixed a very small toddy. Returning to the deck, he sipped the drink and studied the situation broodingly. Finally, "Maybe we could move the shack to the other end. Then it would be Carl's problem. Think it would work?"

Coral jumped off the *Lituya* and walked right up to Bert. There was less than two feet of difference in their height. "Look," she

Toby took off after the sea otter that lives under the raft.

said, peering up at the old man, "if you guys had any sense you'd put the shack in the *middle* of the float. Then you'd know who was responsible for what."

"By golly, I think you've got a point there," said Bert meekly.

"I've got a much better idea," said Vern. "Let's all go aboard the *Dolores* and drink Uncle Bert's booze and forget the whole thing."

"Hear, hear," I said. "A splendid suggestion."

So you see, solving basic engineering problems is really no big thing.

Toby came out of the house and took off after the sea otter who lives under the float. At that moment the friendly creature was sitting on the end of a log, quietly munching on a flounder.

"Hey Toby, wait!" yelled Vern. The admonition came too late. The cat threw all four feet well forward in an effort to stop, but his claws were pointed the wrong way. The otter saw him coming and quietly disappeared under the dock, still clutching his wiggling lunch. Toby had picked up too much speed. Like a drag racer with a split chute, he sailed off into space, spitting and snarling, then gurgled out of sight.

"Hope that cat can swim," said Coral.

He could, and did, and came back aboard angry and puzzled. "I'll get him some day," his expression said as he dragged his wet hide onto the *Dolores.* Bert sat down on the float, crying with laughter.

"You're a nasty old man," said Coral.

We lazed away the warm afternoon, waiting for Carl and Faye to get back from Juneau, and enjoyed the first sun of spring. I sat on deck sketching, and sipped a warm beer. After a few drinks, Bert and Vern got quite serious and figured out how they would move the stranded float. Toby sat outside and washed himself thoroughly of salt water.

About 3:30 the *Patsy* came around the bend. Coral saw the boat first and cried, "Here they come. Now let's get organized. I'm baking a bear roast for supper and I don't want it to burn."

"Oh dear God," Vern said, eyes skyward. "I thought we'd eaten the last of that one already."

"How's bear meat?" I asked innocently.

"Just like yaws," said Vern.

I was puzzled. Finally I queried, "What's yaws?"

124

"Bourbon and water, thank you," howled Vern and everybody laughed.

I had forgotten that old one. After all, the war was over in 1945. Obviously I was the sucker, so I went in and made him a drink.

We gathered around the *Patsy* as Carl and Faye hopped onto the float. "What's new . . . What did the doctor say . . . How are you feeling?" . . . and so on.

"Just call me hot-and-hollow," said Carl. "I've been reamed, punched, bored and blasted. All they found was some kind of infection that caused my cramps. Anyway, a couple shots in the butt seemed to do the trick. Of course I can't sit down. Probably have to sleep standing up."

"He's had enough sitting down to last for weeks," observed Faye. "Their treatment should keep him on his toes for a while."

The tide had already flooded and only a few minutes of slack remained. Vern headed for shore with his kicker while Bert and I hustled across the stretch of water in the *Dolores.* We got a line on the raft and then headed straight out, with Vern shoving. However, the plan had one little flaw. The line parted, just missing Vern as it zapped around the skiff.

We put on a heavier line and tried again. This time the old raft groaned, vibrated and finally let go with a sucking sound. "There she goes," yelled Bert.

I watched as the stern sagged sufficiently to put one corner of the shack awash. "Look out," I cried, "she may capsize."

The old man looked up. "Naw," he said, "she won't. There's plenty of good logs under it yet."

We towed the thing into position and Carl tied it to Vern's float. "Now for some *good* engineering," he said.

Vern had tied a line to the wandering log and it came along with the rest of the mishmash quite obediently. The remaining problem was how to get the thing back under the float.

"Got it all figured," said Bert. He jumped onto Vern's float with a length of line. "Show you how it's done," he said to me.

We poled the log into position beside the float, then the old man wrapped the line around it three times, securing the end of the rope with a staple. Next, Vern walked the rope around the stern, letting it sink slowly, and finally pulled it up on the off-side. "There she is," he yelled. "Bring your boat around, Bert."

They got a fresh log under the float by crude but effective engineering.

The basic idea was to roll the big log under the float by spinning it. We used heavy planks as levers, braced up on Vern's float, with the ends under the other float. Then as we applied our weight, the lopsided float was raised enough to permit the rolling log to slide underneath. As the old man kicked the *Dolores* into full-ahead, the line tightened and the log moved sideways, spinning. Just as neat as you please, it chunked into place. We slacked off our weight on the levers and sat down while the dear ladies plied us with soul-comforting potables.

"How's that for engineering?" Bert yelled, tying up his boat.

"Very crude," I said, "but effective."

"It's a good thing you added those last words," said Vern. "I doubt if you could swim with both cameras around your scrawny neck."

These rugged people make do with anything that's available. Vern, for instance, started felling trees one day. By the end of a week he had enough logs to build a cabin. Within a few days it was fully erected. His tools were a chain saw, an ax, assorted chisels and a hammer. He cut and fitted until everything was locked in place. Now he and Coral live in the cabin, quite comfortably. I wonder how many men could do that today?

The next morning, with a very low tide to assist, the three stalwarts set out to anchor the float. As usual, everything was preplanned.

A rusty, two-inch steel cable was wrestled into place and one end was secured to the starboard side of the float. A nylon rope was attached to the other end, and it in turn was hooked to the *Dolores.* Then we went straight out, letting the cable slop into the water behind us. After some hundred feet we made a wide turn to port, and headed back to the float. "There," said Bert. "That'll hold her for this season."

"Very nice," I commented. "Just one small question. How can that looped cable keep the raft from drifting?"

"Oh," he chuckled, "forgot to tell you. We've got an old lathe laying on the bottom. Must weigh about four tons. We snag the cable around the lathe and bring the other end back to the float. That's all there is to it. Nothing going to move that anchor. And if you'll look astern of the float, you'll see another cable that runs clean ashore. So we're secured on both ends. Got it?"

"Got it," I replied. "However, I was wondering what the red buoy was doing out there in the water. Marks the position of the lathe, huh?"

"Right. When we tie up, ask Vern about that marker. He'll have a story for you."

Vern laughed when I questioned him. "Yeah," he said. "I get tickled every time I think about that." He paused and squinted up the harbor. "See those little red markers down near the old cannery?"

"Yes, I see them. Crab pot markers?"

"Correct. Now according to the law, each one is supposed to have the owner's name painted on. But sometimes a guy will forget or maybe just overlook that requirement. Anyway, the Fish and Game kids come around once in a while and check 'em. If a float isn't marked, they take it up, trap and all."

"I suppose the law must be satisfied."

"You bet. Well sir, one day we were sitting here when Faye says, 'Hey, somebody is messing around with the crab sets.' So we looked over, and sure enough two guys were hauling up pots.

"After a while they wandered up our way. They spotted our anchor marker and over they came. We didn't say anything, just watched, and sure enough one of them grabbed the line and started hauling.

"Pretty soon he says to the other that he needs help. Both of them tried pulling. Course there was four tons of lathe on the other end and it didn't do no good.

"Finally they gave one hell of a yank. All they did was upset themselves. They went into the water with the damndest splash, and we sat here and laughed until we cried. Couldn't help it."

"Then what happened?"

"Oh, they came floundering up and threshed their way to the float. I got stupid and helped 'em get their boat back. Should have let 'em swim all the way back to Juneau."

"Think they got the message?" I asked.

"Sure as hell did. Ain't seem 'em since."

Chapter Fifteen

I had been hearing about Alaskan clams for months: "You've got to get Bert to take you clamming" . . . "You've never seen anything like it" . . . "Clams so thick you don't have to dig 'em. They'll jump in your pail" . . . "Some must weigh two pounds" . . . and so on and on.

Considering that I came from the state of Maine, such stories were ancient stuff. I, too, had dug in many areas untouched by

man, where clams were really clams. The ravings were taken with more than a pinch of salt, and generally ignored.

"We're going to have a four-foot minus tide tomorrow morning," said Bert. "I think we'd better get us a batch of clams. Won't take very long and we can have a real feed."

"Sounds good. Where do we go?"

"Oh, just across the pass to Station Point. There's a little spit over there that's really loaded. I told Carl and Faye to be ready about eight o'clock. We'll drag their skiff along."

Somehow I managed not to fall overboard.

The following morning we set forth to do battle with Alaskan clams. I wasn't too impressed, having dug from the greatest beds anywhere in the world—Down East.

The water was a little choppy and once we nearly lost the skiff. Carl got us stopped in time and snugged up the tow line. Then she rode right on the stern wake with hardly a bounce.

"By golly, I can hardly wait for some clam fritters," said the old man. "Ain't hardly anything as good, not the way Faye makes 'em . . . hey, Carl?"

Faye and I were drinking coffee. "You guys go ahead and praise the cook," she said. "You two still will have to shuck 'em. I'll be darned if I'm going to do that little chore."

"Much sand in them?" I asked.

"No. They live in rocks mostly. Hardly ever get a mouthful of grit. Not like the Eastern variety."

I bristled a little. "You shouldn't knock the East Coast ones, at least not until you've tried them. Why, I've dug clams back there so big you needed a crowbar to get 'em loose. And flavor! Nothing like it. Not a speck of sand." So it went.

"Good thing we wore our boots," I heard Carl say. "It's getting awful deep back there in the cabin."

We dropped anchor about 50 feet from shore. "That's close enough for me," Bert decided. The depth-indicator showed about a fathom, certainly no more, and he considered running aground to be bad manners. The Coast Guard wouldn't understand.

Boarding the skiff proved to be quite an exercise in both balance and reasonably good seamanship. For some obscure reason, neither Faye nor I managed to fall overboard. Carl manned the oars and shouted instructions while Bert watched the operation with a jaundiced eye.

"I think you'd better come back for me" he observed, "if you don't upset first." Thus assured, we headed for shore.

A small causeway, half-moon shaped, extended from a little island to a larger isle. It was covered with rocks of assorted shapes and sizes, none larger than a grapefruit. It was here that the great clam hunt was to begin. Frankly, it did not appear to be clam country to me.

"You'll see," said Faye, grinning.

Juggling two cameras, I floundered onto the beach and looked up and down the causeway. To my surprise, I saw millions of miniature water jets spurting up from the surface, not unlike an upended sprinkler.

"How's that?" yelled Carl, heading back to the *Dolores.*

I looked in awe at a veritable asparagus patch of long, black, waving necks, each one pumping water furiously. I glanced at Faye. She was watching me and laughing.

"Now, smartie, how's that for clams? Ever see anything of the kind in your precious state of Maine?"

"No. I certainly never did. These things must be monsters."

"Oh, I wouldn't say that. Just good sized."

Carl and Bert came ashore, armed with a barn fork and several pails. "Okay, let's get 'em before the tide turns."

Each forkful turned up six to eight beauties and while we scrambled to fill the buckets, Bert took two pails at a time, washed them and stuffed them into a gunny sack. In 10 minutes we had our limit.

Carl took a clam and scooped out a fistful of succulent meat, eating it raw. "Hey," he said, "if I'm not dead by the time we get back, you'll know that this batch ain't toxic."

I like raw clams and oysters but I noticed that Faye shuddered. She said, "Thank you, I'll cook mine. Let's hope there hasn't been a red tide out this way."

"That's why I ate one," grinned Carl. "Somebody has to make a scientific test."

"This wind is really picking up," said Bert. "Let's get the hell out of here before we have to buck our way home."

We were too late. We had to buck and pitch and roll all the way.

"It's okay with me," said the old man. "For anything as good as these clams, we deserve to work a little bit."

When we finally got into the placid waters of Taku Harbor, Toby was storming up and down the float. I translated his yowling: "Where in the hell have you been?"

That afternoon we went over by the old cannery and unloaded Emmett King's groceries. Up to then I hadn't realized how much stuff was crammed in the hold. Must have been nearly a ton and Bert was really wheezing by the time he had passed up countless numbers of cartons. I was puffing too and Emmett and Susie were hard-pressed to keep up with us.

"Ain't there no end to this stuff?" asked King, trying to catch his breath.

Susie laughed. "Here you go sweetheart," and she wrestled off a whole case of cigarettes. "These will help your wind."

We got the boat cleaned out and Bert found six boxes of kitty-litter. "I just knew I'd bought plenty of that stuff. Can't figure why I piled all the groceries on top." Toby looked down at it with approval.

Bert dragged his tired body out of the hold, his glasses steaming in the chilly afternoon air. "By damn, Emmett, take a look at the Plimsoll mark. This boat feels like she's going to pop right out of the water."

Mr. King studied the *Dolores* with great care. "No," he said finally, "I don't think so. Ain't no daylight under her."

I thought the boat did feel a trifle unsteady, so I got down on the float and looked. They both laughed to beat hell.

"That's a gotcha," said Emmett, and Bert cackled, "Might as well check for her barnacles while you're looking!"

You see, it's simple little things like that which cause those dear people to bubble over with mirth.

"I hope your sea-cocks rust out," I said.

Then nothing would do but that we have a few cold beers, and Emmett had to tell me some stories for the "book."

"Guess I never did tell you about the wake for the old Victory Bar, did I?"

"No. As a matter of fact, you haven't told me any stories. One reason could be that I've never seen you before."

"Yeah. You've got a point there. Well it was a real wake. I don't know what brought it on, they lost their lease or something. Anyway, the whole damn bar had to be moved.

"So one afternoon, here comes a regular funeral procession. Must have been a hundred guys lugging stools and tables and chairs, most of 'em was dressed in black or had on armbands.

"And then by god, here comes a coffin, I mean a real coffin, and candles burning and some of the camp followers dressed in veils and silver handles and the whole works.

"Seemed sort of sad, too. They'd hired a guy to beat a drum, all muffled, and the broads was wipin' their eyes and carrying on something awful. One gent has a swallowtail coat and top hat and was carrying a Bible. A real tear-jerker."

"Wait a minute," I said. "What was with the broads dressed in veils and silver handles?"

He glared at me. "I sure wish you wouldn't interrupt when I'm setting the stage. I meant there was real silver handles on the coffin. Ain't you never been to a good wake?"

"No," I said contritely. "I'm afraid not."

"Well sir, the whole parade marches into the new location, where the Victory is now. Everybody sits down and pretty soon a hearse pulls up, loaded with booze. The crowd unloads the carriage and we all went inside and started a good wake. Had the coffin on a table with the candles burning, and old Harry Shultz starts playin' hymns on the piano. Real touching, I thought.

"I don't remember too much after that. Susie says I was drunk for three days. Guess I was. Anyway, somebody paid for it because I didn't have no money when the vigil started and I still had as much when it was over."

"Who was in the coffin?" I asked.

"Don't rightly know. Maybe it was the guy that run 'em out of the old spot. Or maybe there wasn't nobody. I don't know and I don't care, really."

"By golly," said Bert just then, "I hope them bottom boxes of yours are full of canned stuff."

"Why?" Emmett asked.

"Your dog is wetting on every box on the float that ain't more than leg high."

That ended the meeting. We fired up the *Dolores* and went back to our float. About five o'clock Tex and Mildred Hansen came booming in with their new Tollycraft with twin-Chryslers. I guess Tex wasn't quite used to all the machinery because he nearly wiped us out before he got his plaything stopped.

"Look out!" yelled Bert, and we all jumped to starboard and made a grab for the boat.

"Too many throttles and screw controls," hollered Tex.

I started to make a smart remark, but thought better of it. We got a couple plastic bumpers between the boats, and lashed him down securely. I joined the throng that boarded the nice new boat. The skipper, complete with proper yachting attire, welcomed us. "Watch your big feet and don't kick over the beer box."

We visited the bridge and exclaimed over all the goodies. Tex was quite pleased. "Ain't she a thing of sheer beauty? Look at all the levers and buttons and switches, and stuff like that."

They held a real wake for the old Victory Bar.

"Is the auto-pilot electric or hydraulic?" I asked.

"You're damn right!" answered Tex proudly. "Want a beer?"

We all trooped down to the galley. Mildred was scrunched back in a corner, looking tired. "Hello," she said.

Bert couldn't wait. "Hey," he said loudly, "this here is my cook. Say hello to Mildred." So I said hello.

"He ain't really a cook," the old man continued, "he came along to write a story about us fishermen."

Mildred looked at me over a good-sized drink. "You a writer?" she asked finally.

"I'm trying," I answered.

The rest trooped out and Mildred and I talked about writing. I was really pleased at the chance to talk shop with a remarkable woman who keeps Alaska's legislators running scared or honest.

"They're all my friends, though," she said. "I'm a self-appointed watchdog, although that's not exactly what some people call me. I report every cotton-pickin' thing that goes on in the Legislature, and since almost everybody in the Territory—whoops, I mean STATE—reads my stuff, that's one way to keep things neat and clean."

As we built another pair of drinks, she asked, "You really writing about fishing, or what?"

"My original idea was a story of Bert and Toby and the gill-netting business," I told her. "But I prowled around Juneau last week and made some observations . . . I don't know. I realize, of course, that a first-time visitor shouldn't try to write like an expert."

Mildred nodded. "You are right. Leave the necessary muckraking to me or somebody like me, who can blow the whistle and keep it all in the family. We're still going through growing pains up here, things are still kind of raw, but not near as bad as some first impressions might lead you to believe."

She studied me thoughtfully, nibbling the edge of her glass. "No, I really think you should stick to your line of humor and leave the rest to us old pros who have lived here for many years."

Later she sent me a copy of her most recent book, *Handbook For the Freshman Legislator, Or How Not To Be Politically Naive,* and I saw the wisdom of her advice. I recommend that little book highly.

After a while Bert shoved his face inside and bellowed, "Hey, Faye just brought over the clam fritter mix. Come on home and let's have supper."

I said goodnight to Mildred and hopped onto the *Dolores.* It was just in time. Tex had finally found the starter buttons and fired up both engines. Fortunately he crammed them into reverse instead of forward.

"Sure glad we got the lines off," said Bert, staring after him. "Now, let's have a real meal for a change."

We did.

JOE TRA

Chapter Sixteen

EXODUS

It snowed on the hills during the night, down to about the 500-foot level. Outside temperature was nearly at freezing. Once again we had neglected to fill the stove tank. I thought it was getting chilly about 3 a.m. when Toby landed on top of me. Obviously he was cold. Then he tried to run Bert out of his sleeping bag.

We headed out a little after 9 a.m. There were moderate swells in Stephens Passage. Ahead we could see low clouds that promised rain or snow.

We were well up the inlet by 11:30. Carl called and advised there was a lot of trash off Cooper Point. Pretty soon we ran through a long divider, clear water on one side and muddy on the other.

"There's a big river on the off-side of the glacier," said Bert. "It's shoving a lot of dirt right now, and the incoming tide is pushing against the stuff. Must be really wild down below us." He got up and started putting on some heavy clothing. "No use freezing my butt off."

Sitting in the warmth of the wheelhouse, I made a couple of quick sketches of a stream falling from the snowfield. The water tumbled recklessly down the mountain and splashed into the sea. Everything appeared mighty cold to me. Toby looked at my work and then up at the mountain. He refrained from comment. I assumed the work met with his approval. Sometimes it's hard to tell what he's thinking.

"Looks about right to me," said Bert. "But you forgot the seagulls."

The swells were building up and we rolled uncomfortably as Bert poked around looking for a suitable spot for the first set. "Here comes the law," he said. "They'd sure like to catch a net out before noon." The sea-going minions went right on by.

At 12:02 he started the net and at 12:07 the job was completed. The tide seemed to be running in all directions, including up. Bert didn't like the spot.

"Too many boats to suit me. And I don't like this rain either." He shivered a little and filled his coffee cup. "Boy, look at the old weathercock. We'll have to watch so we don't back down on the net." He nudged in a little power, easing away from the corkline, then shut down again.

"Guess we'd better put the stew on to heat. That's all we're going to have until evening. I think we should open that can of ham tonight and really go first class. Been saving it ever since we left Everett."

I worked my way down through a bowl of stew for lunch, scooping off most of the grease. Toby refused to consider even one bite, possibly with good reason.

The old man shoveled his way through several generous helpings, smiling happily. "Best stew I've made in a long time. It'll really stick to your ribs." Looking in the kettle, he shrugged. "Ain't enough to save and it's too good to waste." He poured out the last in his bowl. "You know, you don't eat enough. Bet you've lost a good 10 pounds on this trip. Don't you like my cooking?"

"I sure do, but you've been doing all the work . . . and I cut down on my intake when I'm loafing. I don't want a gut like old Toby."

"Maybe you've got a point there. He *is* getting sort of plump."

"Plump, hell," I said. "He's getting bigger every day. Pretty soon he'll bust."

Toby opened one eye and glared.

"I'm not going to try washing dishes today," I announced. "Don't think there's any way to keep 'em in the sink."

"Okay. Tell you what. We're rolling so damn much I'm going to put the stabilizers down. They won't stop this bucking but they'll take a lot of the snap out."

"Anything to get the dishes done, huh, Bert?"

He grinned. "Not that so much. I just don't want to get pitched overboard when I'm bringing in the net."

"Think we've got some customers?"

"Yeah, I think so. Working in four or five places, we won't get skunked, that's for sure."

At 2:30 we brought in six large kings. "Better than a kick," he yelled. We moved down a quarter of a mile and reset. Then the old man came in, pleased and cold.

"Look at them other boats bunching up on us. They'll do it every time. Just let me get a few fish and look out! Reminds me of flies around a slop-bucket.

"Yes sir," he continued, "that's one thing about this business. Everybody spends their time watching everybody else's nets. Why, if I done that, I wouldn't have time to watch my own. Anyway, I must be lucky. Fish always seem to hop over my way. Same with Carl. Maybe not a lot of fish, but enough. So we don't worry about the other guys—just the seals and sea lions. I've got a damn good surprise for them too. Brought up a whole box of salutes. Boy, when those things bang off . . . well, the seals bang off too, just as fast as they can paddle."

About five o'clock, four more kings came flopping aboard. The wind had settled into a southeasterly blow, snapping whitecaps in all directions. Some snow was appearing in the chilling rain and Bert was half-frozen by the time he cleaned the fish and hosed out the well. He came in shivering and shaking. "Mix me a damn big drink," he commanded. I did so, immediately.

Right after that I opened the can of ham. It being pre-cooked, I thought we could slice and eat as we went along.

"No sir," said Bert. "I'll show you how to really fix up that patch of tinned pig."

Without further ado, he lined a pan with aluminum foil and dumped the whole conglomeration into the container. "This stuff needs to cook more," he assured me. "Now we'll open up some candied yams and then after a while we'll slop on some good canned peas. That's the way to prepare ham."

Frankly, the idea of slopping on canned peas left me sort of cold, principally because I have a violent dislike for the poor, sour, wrinkled, watery, soggy things. But, being a real sport, I went along with such divine guidance.

"Now," said Bert, "she'll be ready to eat about seven o'clock. And I guess I'd better crack some crab for Toby. Poor old cat is falling away to a shadow."

I glanced at the "shadow." It was a fat shadow.

At 6:30 the tide was running one way and the wind another. We drifted onto the net time after time, and after a while the skipper said, "This is no damn good. We're going to foul that net sooner or later, so let's swap ends."

He put a marker buoy on the end at the reel and after disconnecting the lines, dumped everything overboard. Then we bounced around and picked up the opposite end.

"Now, she'll ride better, I hope. I don't like being this close to shore, though, so we'll have to watch out."

For a while things were somewhat smoother. "Guess we'd better eat," commented the old man. "That ham should be just right."

The ham was overly salty, by about 85 percent, and the peas didn't really help. Even Bert agreed that the meat had been a poor selection.

"Don't know how you can tell when you buy 'em," he grumbled. "Maybe I can make pea soup and use it up that way."

"With canned peas?" I asked in horror.

We pulled in four more big kings at eight o'clock. Then Bert studied the shoreline, the water and finally the leaking sky. "Not going to set again, not here. Wouldn't be any use."

"How do you figure?" I asked.

"Oh, I dunno. If I was a fish, I wouldn't work around this area any longer."

Well, that was a scientific answer. So we moved across the inlet to Jaw Point. Carl was just resetting when we arrived. Bert stood off until the net was out, then coasted in beside the *Patsy*.

"Do any good?" asked Faye.

The old man nodded. "Yeah, got about a hundred, I guess. Sort of lost count after a while."

"One-hundred-and-fourteen," I said.

Carl came out on deck. "I figure you overshot your count by at least a hundred."

Bert laughed. "Got about a dozen. How'd you do?"

Captain Nelson smiled expansively. "Five big flounders . . . four small cod . . . three jellyfish . . . two little minnows . . . ."

"And a partridge in a pear tree," I concluded.

"We didn't do much either," Carl confessed. "I'm going to let this set ride for a spell but I don't hold much hope. You going to try here too?"

"Might as well. I figure we'll drift clean out to Admiralty Island the way the tide is running."

We didn't drift quite that far. Instead, Bert reeled in after 20 minutes and said, "To hell with the whole thing."

It was about 11 p.m. when we got the hook out at Troller's Anchorage. The *Lituya* was riding quietly some 200 feet away, completely dark inside. "Guess Vern and Coral have hit the sack," Bert said. "Maybe we should do the same."

"Is this a pretty good bottom?" I asked.

"Sure is. Why?"

"Oh, I got a weather forecast a while ago. Somebody thinks we'll have gale winds tonight and tomorrow, right out of the southeast. I don't believe it though. The glass is steady and this overcast is too thick for anything except steady rain—or snow. Anyway, it doesn't feel like a frontal passage to me."

The old man laughed. "By damn, you're getting pretty good at forecasting. No, we won't get any gale winds. And yes, this is a good bottom. We won't drag the hook in here."

To make up for a sorry dinner, he built a pair of drinks and we relaxed in the quiet waters of the friendly little shelter.

"Old Taku Glacier right up there," he said. "Most people think glaciers are dangerous. In a sense they are, but those big chunks of ice are a part of the world's water supply. Once they're gone, there won't be a solitary place fit to live. Of course you and I won't be around, but it's something to think about."

"It's happened before," I replied. "Another thing, every chart shows the magnetic pole is moving away from the true north pole. The earth is shifting on its axis. Sometime the whole shebang is going to tilt enough to move the ice cap right down to the equator. That's the sort of thing that can spoil a fellow's day."

Bert nodded. "And if it wasn't so late, I'd build us another drink. So you sit and watch the glacier. If she moves, sing out. In the meantime, I'm going to bed."

Again the sadistic alarm started its ringing at 4:30 in the morning. Bert never forgets that monster. An hour-and-a-half later we made the first set directly across from the Scar. While sipping coffee we listened to a few guys bitching about seals grabbing their catch during the night.

The old man laughed. "That's why I didn't set and drift. I sort of figured the damn robbers would be working the night shift."

"I know you talk fish language, but I didn't realize you could palaver with seals, too."

"Oh yes, it's very easy. You see, they only talk about fun and food and sex."

"Just like humans?"

"Exactly."

By 7:30 we went drifting and bouncing past the big rock over by Cooper Point. The tide was rushing in and the wind had shifted to northerly, booming right down off the ice field. It was a bad combination. A number of boats picked up and headed for Juneau.

"That's fine with me," beamed the old man. "Now, maybe we can get to some serious fishing."

I looked up and down and across the inlet. As far as I could see the water was being torn into whitecaps.

"She's blowing a little," said Bert, "but a hell of a long ways from the gales the weather people were talking about last night."

About nine o'clock we went up the Burma Road and made our last set opposite Jaw Point. "Not much use, I guess," muttered Bert. "Still without all that opposition we should manage to snag a few."

We did. Quite a few. But by this time the barometer was starting to drop again and we were both having trouble trying to maintain some semblance of sanity and balance. Finally Bert said, "Oh, nuts, let's go home!"

That took care of that. We reeled in and headed down the inlet.

We got unloaded by mid-afternoon and I was more than pleased to be back in Boat Harbor again. I'd had all the bucking and bouncing and beating I needed for quite some time. I don't know how the gill-netters take it, year in and year out.

"Think you have some story material?" asked Bert the next morning. Emmett was taking me to the Juneau airport and Bert was determined to see that I got there intact.

"Yes," I said, "lots of material. I'm not sure anybody will believe it, though."

Alaska Airlines was right on schedule. We went booming into the cloudy sky at 10:30 a.m. I deliberately selected a seat on the port side, aft of the wing so I could look down on Gastineau Channel as we skirted the city.

Yes, there was the *Dolores* just turning up into Taku Inlet. No mistaking her lines. Mentally I could picture the old man and Toby. I knew they would be looking up at the airliner.

"So long for now, Bert. So long, Toby. Here's wishing you both good fishing."

I could hear Bert saying, "Well, there goes our cook, Toby. Now I suppose you'll be happy. You'll get your own bunk back."

As the airplane turned toward Sitka, I could still see the little boat plowing toward Taku Glacier, bouncing along in the cold, gray water.